For the Living
Selected Writings 1: Longer Poems 1965–2000

RICHARD BERENGARTEN was born in London in 1943, into a family of musicians. He has lived in Italy, Greece, the USA and former Yugoslavia. His perspectives as a poet combine English, French, Mediterranean, Jewish, Slavic, American and Oriental influences.

Under the name RICHARD BURNS, he has published more than 25 books. In the 1970s, he founded and ran the international Cambridge Poetry Festival. He has received the Eric Gregory Award, the Wingate-Jewish Quarterly Award for Poetry, the Keats Poetry Prize, the Yeats Club Prize, the international Morava Charter Poetry Prize and the Great Lesson Award (Serbia). He has been Writer-in-Residence at the international Eliot-Dante Colloquium in Florence, Arts Council Writer-in-Residence at the Victoria Centre in Gravesend, Royal Literary Fund Fellow at Newnham College, Cambridge, and a Royal Literary Fund Project Fellow. He has been Visiting Associate Professor at the University of Notre Dame and British Council Lecturer in Belgrade, first at the Centre for Foreign Languages and then at the Philological Faculty. He is currently a Bye-Fellow at Downing College, Cambridge, and Praeceptor at Corpus Christi College, Cambridge. His poems have been translated into more than 90 languages.

By Richard Berengarten

THE SELECTED WRITINGS OF RICHARD BERENGARTEN
    Vol. 1   *For the Living: Selected Longer Poems, 1965–2000*
    Vol. 2   *The Manager*
    Vol. 3   *The Blue Butterfly* (Part 1, *The Balkan Trilogy*)
    Vol. 4   *In a Time of Drought* (Part 2, *The Balkan Trilogy*)
    Vol. 5   *Under Balkan Light* (Part 3, *The Balkan Trilogy*)

POETRY (WRITTEN AS RICHARD BURNS)
   The Easter Rising 1967
   The Return of Lazarus
   Double Flute
   Avebury
   Inhabitable Space
   Angels
   Some Poems, Illuminated by Frances Richards
   Learning to Talk
   Tree
   Roots/Routes
   Black Light
   Croft Woods
   Against Perfection
   Book With No Back Cover
   Manual: the first 20
   Holding the Darkness (Manual: the second 20)
   Holding the Sea (Manual: the third 20)

AS EDITOR
   An Octave for Octavio Paz
   Ceri Richards: Drawings to Poems by Dylan Thomas
   Rivers of Life
   In Visible Ink: Selected Poems, Roberto Sanesi 1955–1979
   Homage to Mandelstam
   Out of Yugoslavia
   For Angus
   The Perfect Order: Selected Poems, Nasos Vayenas, 1974–2010

For the Living

SELECTED WRITINGS
Volume 1
LONGER POEMS 1965–2000

RICHARD BERENGARTEN

Shearsman Books

Published in the United Kingdom by
Shearsman Books Ltd
58 Velwell Road
Exeter
EX4 4LD

Isbn 978-1-84861-175-7

Copyright © Richard Berengarten, 2004, 2008, 2011

All rights reserved.

The right of Richard Berengarten to be identified as
the author of this work has been asserted by him
in accordance with Section 77 of the
Copyright, Designs and Patents Act 1988.

First published by Salt Publishing, Cambridge, 2004.
Second, hardcover edition, Salt Publishing, 2008.
This third edition, first published in 2011,
contains some textual corrections.

To Melanie

Contents

Editorial Note	ix
Acknowledgments	xi
THE EASTER RISING 1967	1
ACTAEON	15
AVEBURY	23
ANGELS	51
ODE ON THE END OF THE THIRD EXILE	57
NAMING THE CREATURES	65
THE OFFENCE OF POETRY	71
THE ROSE OF SHARON	91
YS	97
TRANSFORMATIONS	105
In Memory of Frances Richards, Painter	106
Dawn	108
Awakening	110
Midsummer	112
Memory	114
Two Lakes	116
TREE	117
DAY ESTATE	131
Matins	133
Lauds	134
Lord's Prayer	135
Antiphons	136

Common Octaves	137
Sexts: Unpunctuated Anthem	138
Suffrage	140
Angelical Salutations	141
Nones	142
Evensong	143
Compline	144
Vigil: Privileged Octaves	146
BLACK LIGHT	147
In Memory of George Seferis (I)	153
The Voice	154
Soulmonger	155
Volta	157
Cicadas (I)	159
Only the Common Miracle	160
Salt	162
Neolithic	165
Song, For Petro	168
Shell	170
Cicadas (II)	171
In Memory of George Seferis (II)	173
Ambassador (An Old Man in the Harbour)	174
MAY	177
AGAINST THE DAY	185
CROFT WOODS	197
VASILISSA	211
Postscript	217
Notes	219

Editorial Note

For the Living is the first volume in the ongoing series of Richard Berengarten's *Selected Writings*. It consists of longer poems and poem-sequences written between 1965 and 2000, in Greece, Italy, England and former Yugoslavia. By and large, contents appear in order of composition, though with several minor departures from chronology. Expanded notes at the end of this edition provide dedications, dates and places of composition, some contexts and references, and details of changes in the choice of poems since the first edition (Salt Publishing, 2004). That edition was published under the name Richard Burns. For the second edition (Salt, 2008), and this third edition, the poet has repossessed his ancestral name.

Acknowledgments

Thanks to the editors who have published some of the texts, whether as books and pamphlets or in collections, anthologies and magazines:

The Easter Rising 1967, poster-poem, *London Magazine*, January 1968; Restif Press, Brighton, 1969; and *The Return of Lazarus*, Bragora Press, Cambridge, 1971. 'Actaeon', *New Measure* 4, Oxford 1996–7; and *Double Flute*, Enitharmon Press, London, 1972. 'Angels', poster-poem, Los Poetry Press 1977, 1979, 1983; *Voices Within the Ark*, The *Modern Jewish Poets*, Avon Books, New York, 1980; *Learning to Talk*, 1981; *Roots/Routes*, Cleveland State University Poetry Center, 1982; and *Against Perfection*, King of Hearts, Norwich, 1999. 'Ode on the End of the Third Exile' and 'Naming the Creatures', *Learning to Talk*, Enitharmon Press, London, 1981. *Avebury*, Anvil Press Poetry with Routledge & Kegan Paul, London, 1972; and *Shearsman* e-book, August 2003, http://www.shearsman.com. 'The Offence of Poetry', *Littack IIII*, Epping, 1973. 'The Rose of Sharon', poster-poem, Los Poetry Press, 1974, 1983; poster-poem, *Learning to Talk*, 1981; and *Roots/Routes*, 1982. 'Ys', *Poetry Wales*, January 1978. 'Transformations', *Lines Review*, Edinburgh, March, 1989; 'Awakening', *With a Poet's Eye*, Tate Gallery, London, 1986, 1993; and 'Two Lakes', *Book With No Back Cover*, David Paul, London, 2003. *Tree*, Menard Press, London, 1981; *Roots/Routes*, 1982; and *Against Perfection*, 1999. *Black Light*, Los Poetry Press, Cambridge, 1983 and 1986; The King of Hearts, Norwich, 1995; and selections in *Against Perfection*, King of Hearts, 1999. 'May', *The Jewish Chronicle*, 16 August 1991; and *Against Perfection*, 1999. 'Against the Day', *Against Perfection*, 1999. *Croft Woods*, Los Poetry Press, Cambridge, 1999; and *Against Perfection*, 1999. 'Vasilissa', *Tremblestone*, Plymouth, 2004.

Thanks also to: Rachel Paterson and Rhiannon Gooding for permission to reproduce the watercolour by Ceri Richards on the front cover ('Memorial to Dylan Thomas', 1954), and the four lithographs from *Les Illuminations* (1975) by Frances Richards which accompany 'Transformations'; to the Royal Literary Fund and the David Garrard Educational Trust for generous material support; and, finally, to Anthony Davies, Melanie Rein, Angus Calder and Joanne Limburg for their invaluable textual criticisms and advice on finer points of selection and ordering.

RB
CAMBRIDGE
JULY 2008

The Easter Rising 1967

I

I am sick of the twittering of swallows' voices,
My Lord, I have come down from the North
To find only You, but sitting by the well
I was assaulted by perfumes
And the babbling of a thousand animals
Performing the rites of Spring. I am sick to death
Of them all, My Lord,
You do not walk among them.

II

The army has taken over the state
Lord   I am sick
Citizens are forbidden
To gather in groups of more than five
For the safety of all citizens
The king is chewing his nails in the palace
His signature has been faked
Tanks patrol the city streets
And half the people's ministers are in prison
Including three past premiers
Citizens are forbidden
To walk outside their houses
The constitution has been suspended
By the order of the army and the police
Civil crimes will be judged under martial law
For the safety of all citizens
Newspaper   radio   telephone   telegraph
And all forms of transport and communication
Have been suspended
No one shall enter or leave the country
Any citizen seen on the streets after dusk
Will be shot on sight
For the safety of all citizens
We shall discover a communist plot tomorrow
And concoct a suitable scapegoat
Citizens are forbidden
To criticise the regime
By the order of the army and the police
Lord   I am sick

For the safety of all citizens
Citizens are forbidden
Citizens have been suspended

III

The green corn grows but the poppies grow higher
And other red memories spatter the fields
The shepherds are bringing their flocks from the hills
Down into town for the Easter slaughter
The women have painted the house fronts white
The peasants wade knee deep in green corn
But the blood of the poppy covers the land
A shepherd who had not heard the news
Came down into town after dusk and was shot
The lambs are brought down for the Easter slaughter
And my firstborn son is a conscript now
The blood of the poppy covers the land
Other red memories spatter the fields
Must I live through them all over again
Lord   I have been drunk all day
But I am sick to death of it all

IV

In martial formation the swallows returned
They came with the tourists   all twittering
But they have brought us no news
They sing for themselves and hear no one else
They are afraid for their lives
They chatter in high pitched foreign dialects
And I cannot understand a word that they say
Lord all our newspapers are ten days old
The neighbours have told the police
That my cousin is a guest in my house
Lord they have confiscated my rifle and his
We shall hunt no more the hares on the hills this year
Lord I hear the summer flies buzzing
They interfere with every other sound
Lord the shit in the shithouse is piled up to the ceiling
And no one so strong as to clear it away
All the radio stations screech in foreign languages
I have twiddled the knobs all day
My friends are all afraid to speak to me
To whom shall I turn
Lord   I do not know what is happening
Lord   I am sick
These foreigners   these barbarian swallows
How cruel is their oblivious song
They are speaking about us   I know
But I am not immune like them
Lord   I am sick
Help me

V

    Theodorakis
Who composed the beautiful dances and songs
    Papandreou
Who fought for a vote for each man
Unrigged elections
Pensions and better education
    Kanellopoulos
Who led the last government
    Glezos
Who won a prize for peace
And so the story goes (apocryphal or not)
Climbed the Acropolis
To plant the Greek flag instead of the Swastika
While the Nazis murdered our women and children
And the S.S. sprawled in Merlin Street
An idiotic schoolboy gesture
That gave our hearts fresh blood
    Spyridoula
Who has a shop in the high street
Which sells stoves and cylinders of calor gas
    Sotiriou
Who lost an arm in the war at the age of seventeen
    Pappageorgiou
Who drives a lorry
Whose son is my son's friend
    Ploumbis
Who played backgammon with me last week

Where are they now?
Where are they now?

Neigh for them
Till the cows come home

Are we
Or they
Imprisoned?

VI

And I am sick of the song of the military
The captains who strut like pigeons down the street
Having just been promoted
And the raucous laughter of beardless conscripts
Parading in the market place
    With wolf whistles and dirty jokes
    And swearwords cram-full of innocence
    And tanks outside the post office
    And tommy-guns outside the electricity board
    And bayonets fixed outside the telephone exchange
    Stopping the traffic on the highways
    Arresting people in their homes
    Publicly picking up whores below the Acropolis

They do not understand
I am sick of people who do not understand
Because they are innocent
I am sick of innocence

And I am sick of the smiles of friendly policemen
Whose eyes betray their fear of being removed
From their meagre wages and wives and mothers
They too are innocent

And I am sick of the cowed silence of peasants and shopkeepers
Who want peace and quiet at any price
I am sick of them because they are right as usual
I am sick of watching their foreheads furrowed by worry
The complaints of their whispering women
The puzzled uncertain eyes of their children
The silence punctuated by forced laughter in the coffee houses
And bars and taverns where men cannot talk as they please

Lord I am sick of the rich
Washing their cheeks and turning the other hand
Of dowagers with face-lifts learning peasant dances
Surrounded by troupes of performing lesbians and ponces
Concerned with their make-up and sun-tan on the beaches
Who own smoky factories in Eleusis
Who have never been to Eleusis

They are all innocent
But I am sick of innocence
Lord I have lost my delight
In the cherry tree in the garden
I am sick of the apricot and almond and artichoke
And the smell of the lilac has turned to shit in my nostrils
And yellow sweet retsina tastes like urine
Oh God I am sick of the conversation of all my friends

VII

For six nights on end I have been stinking drunk
On ouzo beer and wine in every bar in town
And I have not found one man to whom I could open my heart
Lord I have no newspapers
The state has cut out my eyes
Lord the radio tells lies
Between all my favourite songs
My ears are filled with cement
Lord my friends are afraid to talk to me
The police have sold my tongue in the market for dog food

Where there is language
There is no exile

Lord I am exiled
In my own land

VIII

Announcement
It is forbidden
For more than five fleas to congregate together after dusk
It is forbidden
For more than three chairs one cigarette stub and two beer mugs
To be found loitering together
It is forbidden
For women to fuck more than five men in one evening
Except officers
Who do not count
Who cannot count
It is forbidden
For officers' wives to menstruate
Because it is a semi-barbarous custom
It is forbidden
For virgins under the age of sixty-nine
To wear skirts more than one millimetre above the knee
It is forbidden
For men to have hair
And all schoolchildren will shave their heads like convicts
It is forbidden
To look in another man's eyes
Except with the aid of a powerful electric torch
It is forbidden
To use swearwords like Liberty
It is forbidden
To dream

IX

I have dyed two dozen eggs for Easter
Blood red   My Lord   blood red
I have bought a white fleeced lamb in the market
Weighing fourteen kilos
The prettiest creature ever born for sacrifice
And I have carried it home over my shoulders
And now I hear it bleating
Tomorrow it will be slaughtered
Lord   I pray do not pass over my house
I am ready for you when you come
Lord   I am sick of the blood of the lambs
Redder than cochineal

Do not pass over my house
Lord   I am ready

Actaeon

No fanciful townwit can

Tell in skilled story

The truth of my longing

Famous in legend

I sang like the cuckoo

The maidens turned round

Come away Come away

Measure my mettle

My keenness of bow thrust

Actaeon my name

When I rode on the fields

My voice made men jealous

When I laughed at the peasants

Bright were my eyes

In pools I saw your image

Lissome white lady

You haunted my haleness

With dream delirium

Pockmarked my young face

Everywhere I saw you

But in the city

I set out to seek you

Lithe fallow deer

Shadow, bright butterfly

You harrowed my hunter pride

Shuttered my sight

With the blindspot of venery

Nightlight and daylight

Where most I sought you

I brushed you in bracken

By brackish waters

Grazed you in fern fronds

And air pawing blind, held

Only the valley lily

I turned at your shadow

Below the tree shadow

With red wounds bruised black

Finding never

Your scent in my nostrils

Blown by the breezes

But saw my own shadow

In terror I shot it

Fine was the forest dare

Dispelling the dark fear

Which haunted my hunting

Dizzy as wine draughts

My flesh knew the tree bark

The hornsong borne hollow

And angry birds wheeling

Hunting your music

Of dream delirium

The hunt was my music

Sweeter than evensong

My ear heard the hounds bark

In the echoing valley

At the perilous kill

In the horn you called me

From the flesh of women

Come away Come away

To the flashing of livery

Between the green trees

Come away Come away

To the great deer's antlers

Come away Come away

Far from the city

You sang in the wine flask

Redder than blood

To the streaming manes

To the doe's red blood

Come away Come away

My sterling companions

The saddle and bridle

Leather I loved

In the darkest forest

Black stag and hind

And roebuck and mottleback

Till I saw the white lady

The basset and bloodhound

And the bow I swore by

Swift were my arrows

I hunted the hart

Those fleeing animals

Haunted my dreams

Lost in the city

In the heart of the city

I heard great bells ring

Darker than evensong

Come away Come away

From the cavernous forest

Of basset and bloodhound

For the last time

I saw the lithe fallow deer

Clearer than judgement

She called me by name

But I heard my own echo

Sing in the wine flask

I raised my bow

I slew the white lady

Go village bred minstrel

Sing on your harp

With harvest wine flask

Where the wind whispers

Spanning the valley

Yearning to hunt me

In the bracken bound forest

Tell peasant women

Around warm fires

How I who am dumb

Lost my high laughter

To the doe in the city

But hear their black laughter

Where I walk in tree shadow

Power was mine when

I sang as the cuckoo

From the heart of the city

Come away Come away

Now the maidens mock me

Lithe fallow deer

Shadow my shadow

My name was Actaeon

Traitor to women

I ruined the harvest

When I look in the pools

Now I see my own image

Where once before

White lady, I saw yours

Avebury

for Octavio Paz

To rise up and become wakeful guardians of the living and of the dead.

HERAKLEITUS OF EPHESUS

And the Lord shall be King over all the earth; in that day shall the Lord be One and his Name One.

SABBATH MORNING SERVICE

For the first time in our history we are contemporaries of all mankind.

OCTAVIO PAZ

I

    huge slabs
wrenched
from under grass, dug
    out of hills

               time's
                teeth

                worn

         yawning the sky in

           porte of light

earthed

    tongued

                broken
                altars

           answerless

covered the cave's
cracked jaw

II
            back and forth
                round and round
under the cloudy dome speechless

sniffing among these petrified hopes
        these ossified dreams   these
            dead memorials   pacing
            back and forth

    ancestorless

under the compact slogans of the sky

                walking
                as dead

    cursing
        their answers
        their meaning

looking for what

                    the riddle?
                    the question?

III

and can the stone know
me   I wonder
  does the stone
         wonder

even here   among absences
and wreckage

   if any place

IV

        if any place
        most of all

here, most
of any

       in the dance
in the ring
    of stones dancing
metaphor on metaphor
            silence
                anagrammatised
measured   spaced out
     in this syntax of land
  this plot of time

where the green causeway ends
where the avenue ends
where thought ends

       begins
           the burial
         the dance
                    of stone
    begins

V

    the sky's throat
    says

Ascend Sun

from this syntax of hills
    this plot of space

        mean

    light

ripples
expanding
    across the downs
        waves returning
  from where? the centre
to where? circumference

      now any
       place is now

        say the stones

I do not tell   *I say*

VI

      little mother
of Willendorf
         'vegetable' Venus
   of the hunters
         neckless head
   featureless
       under the beehive hair
thin arms asleep   on breasts
         like hills   belly
   enormous   the buttocks
steatopygous   the whole blind body
     bowed over the womb
   as if above
    an unseen child

VII

      in the gallery
contorted   struggling
      The Prisoners
  one in limbs and torse
          nigh perfect, yet
   with genitals
           trapped
under unhewn rock
        the arms
    unable to heave
  backbreaking
      stone off his head
   undiscovered
        dreaming in

VIII

      and at Samothraki
striding out   came dancing
        Nike
     the daughter

              headless
in the wind   and taking wings
   her robe a river of hair
over the jutting curve of her
      incredible arrogant breasts

     and the breakers
         confluent
   under the belly
    forming   like an unseen hand
protecting her cave   the mouth of her

IX
      on snake island
two *phalloi*
         unsheathed from stone like flowers
                and the air parched
                        so high above the sea
that time of year, August
               with *Meltemi* blowing
and an hour by boat back to Mykonos

               poised erect
                     twin offerings
                twin motives

     one of the shafts
broken
    above the marble scrotum

    X

       now see where in marble play
            the musicians: a sturdy
flautist with double pipes
                stuck in his chinless face
his companion seated at a cracked harp

   nameless the song   from a cave by the sea

                silence

        still growing
       out of,   louder

  heads uptilted   blinded by sunlight

        the tune climbing, still
         going strong in

great dusky sea, so many pebbles round your neck
  so many glinting jewels in your hair

XI
>   I am awake
>   sleeping, I wake

in
the cave, tomb
   and temple

>   under
>   turrets that wind
>   and climb

>   deep in your chambers

where I lost my memory
        of concerns and imports
           and the way
           up is way
             down

   of all but boyhood

                those dead children

    ghosts

I said
I never believed in

               you
           here, all present?

XII

down the corridor wound like a horn
and not a glimmer
                to the first signs
half a mile in from the surface
you touch but don't believe,
nor shadow of a glimmer down beyond them
   your eyelids
                jumping like fish
veil nothing here: you are the very
     shadow you discarded

                all is eyes

      your path
   a spiral groped along, past
cataracts of stalactite
   stalagmite screens, chasm
      waterfalls, chimneys, columns
                    and with a twist
   upwards through a manhole
         sides worn smooth

into the gigantic halls
                the
          know not where

Light,

    and your hands
    a sudden shield a torch
    shaking out shadows

        against a blaze of inner noon
        your blindness

you

    there, my
    sister? my brother?

pounding
of blood across temples

        breath
        an instant held

    the drip
    drip of distant water

that unfathomable roaring

XIII

        where sleeps the man
who shaggy haired
    roamed the steppes
          with wolf and bison
      ate grass, and played
           with the herds

                in *that time*

  before she came
        with her ear-rings
of amber   her breasts bared
    her armpits scented
  let down her braided hair
and struck you with that gaze of stone
  taught you the art of her stone smile
      woke you with language
    of cattle
  byre and cave

    I am awake
    sleeping, I wake

                in *that time*

     before Delilah

XIV

   and where now

    brother of boyhood
   male half of my otherness
    strong as the beasts you hunted with
before we hunted

   how have I lost you
in this cave blackness   dancing
  blinded by a mask of hands
        in *that time*
    by my own cunning

    changed my face
    like one gone
      under sunlight
    on a long journey

aye we must treasure the dream whatever the sorrow

    brother, you
   were the axe at my side
     my hand's strength
    the sword in my belt

       in *that time*

  standing in this cave of light
    this mouth of stone
   that eats me

XV

words you rush in on me like a surf
into my core like semen to the uterus
like torchlight on these stones
moving and melting the frost's shadow behind them
trebling their din with intervening silences

and who is this come riding
in on the foam this long haired
green creature who brings me
back again among the scattered seasons

once I was young enough to think
you like these stones were immortal

in the wave that gathers you up in it like a sandgrain
and drops you down somehow else,
                              has it changed you, the sea?

has it turned you into a fish? a note? a pearlseed?
in the silt did you taste like thi?
whose was it that kiss,
                 who was it embraced you?

      jetsam of dream,
      eroded

down in the pit I have seen your face   mother
  your skull in the rockface

           and who is that other
              face in shadow
           the cloud that lurks just behind you?

XVI

    stone
    you too

    a monad

    atom
        as I am

what is the sum
of these quanta?

        I am not just
        my body

    are you
        stone
    my body?

the total?

XVII

under my eyes   these stones
            are

                 dancing

                       stars

                               birds

         figures of speech

growing into each other
                out of each other

    and have become
the spaces   between them

                           points
                 in the dance

           including me
             enclosing me

me, embraced
    in this dance of stone

XVIII

stone in me
stone that I am
centre or periphery
nomad and society of atoms

    eyed by stone
    eaten by stone
    loved by stone

danced in the dance
    by the dance
      of stone

by stone
    uttered
by stone
    dreamed

XIX

bloody stone
   blood I am
grained
   with breath
death of ancestors
    of my blood
  stone I am

wizened

   enduring

      the sun's hammer
      the frost's nails
      the wind's arsenal

XX

adamant

    defying discourse
        messages
eyes   tongues

    telling nothing
giving nothing
      being of absence
core   the dream

    threshold
      ledge of energy
meniscus of darkness
    grain of light

    bringing to life
in me what does not exist
me in what does not exist

        subversive stone

    uprooting
    word from language

winding down
    time to rubble

        this continuum

    in you

all is the saying

XXI

in my throat
the man rises
    from the cave he was immured in

        break
    speech
in a tide on these stones
        wash
clean   break
    word
into stone
    out of stone

        sleeping, I wake
        I am awake

    and the ghost gone at end
    of childhood

comes back
eroding, endures

    among these ancestors

        sharing

XXII

in the neat but functional lines
                        of Block H
in the beige walled waiting room
                        of The Labour Exchange
in the public bar of The Tiger
                    or The Square and Compasses
in the new auditorium
                  of The College of Arts and Technology
in the Maplan Supermarket
      that sells everything

                who rent out
            a plot of elements
              who lodge in
                    seams of space
        with just room to move
           from corner to corner
          in a web of gravities
                thick as a word
              shimmering
           on a beam of time
                bound there
                    to say out

from what is between these hands
from what is under these eyes

ancestors' fathers
locked in stone
we struggle out of
measuring
immeasurables

XXIII

this was no whore
   not abandoned
not 'wild'
   and cruel only

   when an absence
and no gap
   between speech and her mouth

     matter of words
     word of matter

   always touch
lips touch
                speech
tongues   the world
   born

       wherever

   light of eyes
   eye of light

child of elements

   wherever
        touch and find

anywhere centre

          say these stones
          of Avebury

XXIV

find any
where centre

        echoes from peripheries
        out of galactic range

        creatures awake on distant shores
        across those seas and skies

        beyond sidereal thoughtspan back
        to breathing

                waves
                expanding, re-echoing

including
us here

enclosing
us here

    say the stones

now every
where centre

        I do not tell   *I say*

Angels

We were a multitude, until the hunters,
scouting the immemorial pastures
with hewn weapons, on foot and horseback,
tracked us down where we ambled grazing
and fell upon us with poisoned javelins,
picking us off, first one by one,
then scourging by hundreds as they closed in,
burning, smoking us from the homelands,
hounds baying, snapping our heels,
till, blood-glutted, gorged on our meat,
wearing our hides, copying our calls
and rubbing our fat, death-scented,
into their flesh to charm and ensnare us,
in droves ambushed, for blood smell only,
as if to wipe out a hunger for hunger
by slaughtering, to become us, to be us,
their glazed eyes deep, ice-covered pools
where our charred valleys were drained moistureless
and our own murders measured and mirrored,
and we scattered to barren tundra.
And there evolved. In full light and day ebb
and utter darkness, warily through every
season, kept watch, and by winds smelled them,
learned their shadow shapes and cunning
and when to rush through the closed circles
of their web-knit formations that hemmed us in
amid moving henges of hurlers and missiles
and, leaner, hardened, lighter-footed,
wove secret speech of our own.
But on they harried us, overtaking
infants and aged as they fell back,
hacked off limbs, and what was left

of crippled mutilated bodies
hung for trophies on bark-stripped poles,
while we who still had strength enough
fled through the few remaining trees,
stumbled aimless over moors and heathland
into deserts to die of thirst, hid
in caves and were lost in their windings
under bleak hills, or perished in forests
beyond borders of the known world rim.
We who survived, ten, twelve, sixteen,
now wild in willpower and aware of destiny,
waking more sternly with each weary step,
came out of despair and to land edge
and plunged for refuge in deep waters
under the ice floes. And six or seven died
frozen or drowned, and there were no more
young. Lungs afire for want of air,
the rest swallowed, held on, swam deeper,
limbs attuning to water's rhythms,
building fat under newly sealed pores,
muscles till now unused growing firmer,
breath longer, blood beat slower,
the whole skin another ear drum,
eyes widening to take in darkness.
Self-delighting in a borrowed world,
slow to learn grace, we received as a rite
water's gift, laughter, that drowns weeping
and engulfs memory of all time but presence
which, itself a flood, buoyed us up
to sing across aeons, and our long calls
spanned oceans' depths and embraced the other
depths we embraced in and through one another,

till our speech took on the pitch and resonance
memory's currents had eroded in us
wound round the endless whorls of the sea.
And so multiplied, grew sleek and lazy,
vast in girth, living only for music,
when their sensors picked up our frequencies.
Then slaughter was unstinted and our cries,
churning placid waters, hammering the soft
inverted womb the seas had become, whose walls
we beat on, numbing last strengths uselessly,
jammed their tracking instruments as too late
remembering a nightmare from another
world, or other existence, again we woke
and dragged their bucking vessels leashed behind us
across the waves' vertiginous surface. Then blood
stained estuaries and caked whole coastlines
where our hauled wrecks were carved and heaped
in messes on the beaches, till the creeks stank.
Then we were few: three, perhaps, four.
To zones unhaunted, by no fish followed,
where water's weight and sheer blackness
pressed till we shrank and merged with shadows,
down we dived, deeper than terror.
Then we were two, and we sang each other
of Tiphareth, of the Throne, of the Glory.
Indescribable our lamentations,
we, the uncounted, the unaccountables,
sons and daughters of the starry heavens
become a lost calling without a name
drifting among unfathomed valleys,
until I called, recalled, and heard
no answering song. Then quietly I climbed

and on a still sea trumpeted, took air
and dived for ever. And you'll not find me
nor you nor you, till the almond tree flowers
on the mountain, and there is no more sea.

Ode on the End of the Third Exile

I

Bearer of the double flute among those hill walled cities,
through villages hive crowned, smelling of resin and thyme
and the swallows going barmy in their ivy hung eaves,
in wood stacked fishing hamlets precarious on estuaries,
breezing into valleys of silvering olive trees,
down trellised slopes, vine thick, murmuring with bees,
on lizard tracks out again, through harbours of deafening
evening cicada choirs, stung witless by mosquitoes,
seven whole years I tramped that alien peninsula,
inland, swamp and coastline, intent on my business,
missionary for Dionysos, marketer of ecstasy.
and there hoisted altars, built statues of local stone,
wove spiral mazes for feet of dancing celebrants,
at marriages and funerals sang against all comers,
promoted festivals in name of Pan and Orpheus,
in tired skulls planted grains gathered from Mnemosyne
and broke decaying certainties in tides bearing Aphrodite.
their princes showered gold on me, ornaments, brooches,
no minor official reserved his praise in irony
but sweated hospitality free from a full purse
till I massed fame and riches, proper reward of poets,
grew dolphin-sleek and lazy, whiskered like a sea lion,
squandered it, all of it, to brothel and pornshop keepers,
and one blue domed morning when the light chimed on the air
left on foot for the isthmus, with just my fare for the voyage.

II

And as my ship Hesperus rode out beyond the capehead,
the waves' mist-shrouded surcoat was a veined filigree sheen
set with opals and diamonds, a rich hoard of illusions,
and a hag hung on the light, horrible in her beauty,
plucking dismal chords from a battered heart-shaped instrument,
her pearly body hovering, swaying with the ship's tilt
leeward, seeming to smile at me, immune on the grey air
like a cloud muffled moon, as though we were dancers frozen
immutably in partnership in a sculpture of stone.
Among wheeling gulls and cormorants, I alone could see
her shimmering eyes, dangerous, large orbited, whirlpools,
toothless jaws and sunken cheeks under lank uncombed white hair,
high-waisted body, naked, firm fleshed, small breasted, beautiful,
and above the timbers' creak and whining of sails in wind,
lapping and whisper of waves, birds' comments, interruptions,
crewmens' drunken curses and scurry to obey orders,
I alone could hear her, I alone knew the air she sang,
searing and charring my brain, pouring ash down my spine,
beckoning to me, Sleeper? When will you arise again?
laughing at me, leering, to dive in the waters after her,
summing all voices of all women I had ever loved,
ever longed for, despaired of, hated, fled from in terror,
and my legs caved under me and I crept below decks
where among barrels and baskets, cocooned by the cargo,
under the hatch I lay as drowned in forgotten ages.

III

Three times from my dream's whirlpools her sea green voice came again,
'What does this mean, o sleeper? Arise, call on your god. This
ship shall sink under morning, and shall you drown among them?'
And I groaned under the weight of it, and cried, 'No, I am mortal,
a mere daytime creature, warm child of noons and dawns.' And she:
'This heart I pluck is yours. Shall only this remain
untouched after cremation when your companions find you,
a bloated mangled wreck spewed from the ocean's belly,
or shall we watch this night out and untwine the net of time?
Come now, breathe with me undersea, or drown beneath the morning.
Between passion and action a twin-stranded thread is spun.
One strand is fate, one destiny. At the last waking, choose.'
'I am a singer,' I answered. 'A dancer. No saint. No madman.'
And three times, at watch changes, the crewmen, jeering, roused me
out of sleep's forgetfulness, dragged me on deck, clamouring,
'Is this not the loafing minstrel, famous in our country,
inventor of the maze dance, pimp of princess and priestess,
great drinker and brothel louse, travelling incognito?
Fantasy haggler and barterer. Mimic of accents.
Night croaker. Toad that snores day out, but does no true man's work.
Daughter and wife seducer. Corrupter of our children.
Is this not the fellow, who now brings the storm demons down?'
'See my clothes, my purse,' I said. 'I am a poor traveller,
I too fear death by drowning, I too am a man like you,
my voice is as yours and we cannot compete with the sea.'

IV

The third time they hauled me out, an hour or so before dawn,
the mist was gone and the thick sea roared its foul crescendo,
and out of my dream's waves, out of the eye of the sea storm,
again I saw her eyes, again I heard her beckoning,
plucking my heart strings faster, wilder, until I coughed blood,
while they saw nothing, heard nothing, only the bitter sea,
and cried to their gods to save them, to let them live the day,
as they threw more stuff overboard, until all ballast was gone
and the strangled morning light battled the clouds above us.
Then, eyes aglint, fear sharpened, they pinned me to the side,
'Toad, who can call up storms, are you not a sea demon yourself?'
And they drew daggers and muttered, 'Is this not an Hebrew?'
till the thoughts of all those frightened men sprouted a single head,
'Save us with a song, fat Hebrew, or we throw you overboard.'
But their arms that held me grew small, all fear abandoned me,
I laughed through that dawnless morning, and a huge breath
                                              filled my lungs,
'Now turn me to a tadpole, make me my father's seed
afloat in the womb of the sea, till my lungs shrink to gills.
I hear songs other than your songs, see sights other than yours,
I have a voice to carry me aeons under the sea,
I am the man you look for. Now do with me what you will.'
'Toad,' they said, 'Foul Hebrew. Go marry your bitch of a mother.'
'Poet,' they said, 'Betrayer. Drink your milk of paradise.'
'Liar,' they said, 'Coward. Be joined with your bastard father.'
And they threw me into the sea, which closed round about me.

V

The water surrounded me wholly, even to my core.
The depth closed round about me. Its weeds were wrapped round
                                               my head.
I went down to the roots of mountains. The earth with her bars
was about me. And I was unknowing, dark, of the dark.
I breathed billowing water, tasted and touched salt sweetness,
trod and walked water, became the companion and comrade
of round-eyed, slit-eyed creatures whose element is ocean.
I was a crab, a squid, an octopus, an anemone,
a silver shoalfish, scavenging, a lone shark, a hunter,
I sang among whales, I leaped and rolled with dolphins,
learned their subtle languages, rhythms, wavelengths, melodies,
inhuman, wordless, yet meaningful, until I remembered
the maze dance, and hungered for men and women again,
the clasp of hands, words, eyes, nets and songs of fishermen,
children's laughter, pipers and drummers of the northern isles
who, despite death, know there is no bitterness in the sea.
And then I wept, agelessly, and a creature with green eyes,
wide orbed, shimmering, whirlpools, and warm blood in her body
spoke to me in my mother tongue, 'Son of earth, sky breather,
enough of sea and weeping. Now it is time to return.
with clarity and patient love all things come to ripeness.'
and over the waves she bore me, on her back, past islands
floating like cloud shadow on the surface of the waters
and left me on this shingle, a shell to be filled by air.
Now I stand, and hear waves lapping. I stand on my own feet,
and I go north, to cities, to work for love and justice.

Naming the Creatures

He could not see what flowers were at his feet.
    He could not see what flowers. And yet, by guessing, named.
And through that space he cleared, amid the may and wood,
    we chased conditions he had never claimed.
Glades overhung with ivy, overgrown. What wine,
    his dream of dying and his dying dream had blurred
echoed right round us, though what we overheard
    was not his creatures singing, but an obscure complaint
as of alien musicians, plucking rhythms whose design
    bled like wind, wordlessly, unheeding all constraint.

What living things we recognised, what dignities redeemed
    lay in their true calling. Their scent lay in their names,
their music and strength also. What he, half drunk, had dreamed,
    or seemed to dream, or half dreamed, revealing, was their names,
and what lies still unnoticed among the eglantine,
    woodbine, etcetera, as background hum, absurd,
crackling its interference around each uttered word
    is feared, denied, ignored, for being adrift and strange
till, seeing or unseeing, a sayer makes the sign
    which moves us to its perspective and focuses it in range.

And we have gone out walking with our loved ones and kin
   who share those creatures' voices, and can name each flower and tree,
     and when, through their naming, unbidden song pours in,
  open, in wordless rhythms, undistorted, free,
we have recognised and listened, and unfamiliar zones
   have flowered through unclenched hands between the things we knew
and called us to them, welcoming, and we've gone in, and through,
   and named each new born creature with a loved one's special grace.
But where are those names written? In our heads? our hearts? our bones?
   And how can we protect them, there in that green space?

In the song that bereaves its hearer but still thrives,
   the singer maintains silence. Who then is it utters
what he could not see, but named? What is it survives
   in us, of that naming? And what breath lifts and mutters
to this tangle of riotous growth its hidden order?
   Harnessing the creatures to keep them safe and tame
turned them against us, and they escaped in all but name,
   or we left them, half throttled, on chartered, vacant ground,
till nothing seemed worth claiming on that disputed border
   between inner and outer mists, muteness and raucous sound.

Must the creatures lie breathless there? Is there no redeeming
   the world we would capture within the poem's snares?
Must we be evaded, cheated in veils of seeming,
   incapable of rising to the green song that dares
us on, through language, not just from the next glade
   nor even the afternext (which tempts us overmuch),
but here, from this world, the unnamed we see and touch,
   the never-yet-noticed in what we take for real,
this bird, *this* flower, the life of *this* grass-blade,
   this, the universe I'd have our names reveal?

Universe unseen, in hunting which were haunted
   by this, your truth, illusion, your cry of hope, your shout
promising inheritance, following undaunted,
   wherever we escape, whether inside or out,
you: we: names: world: flower: nightingale,
   who *are* those hunted creatures, sayers, seers and hearers,
whole, hollow within and without, stringed instruments and bearers:
   we name the names of names, where all see, all is seen,
and are your creatures' namers, although defining fail,
   by naming, we reveal what condition these names mean.

The Offence of Poetry

Is no beginningness

Obscured, the white target of saying: here, there, gone. Clouded among speculations, serial apparitions, shifts in the seeing, dispersals in the seen,

the rainbow dissolves in transparency, and the bird's quick call, hollow silence. Out there, above the surface of the dream this swims through,

music, unremembered, is playing in an other silence. I dream I hear it, and dream I am waking. But its still moment flown towards stretches back infinitely,

and forward, also infinitely. Absence, that moment's sediment, lies thick on every second: its gravities muffle the utterance.

And distracted by its reflections, inaccurate these aims: always short of the mark, plummeting back in the dream,

their spiral tracks decomposing into drifting random particles, parabolas distorted into telling and evanescence,

between these wavering margins of remembrance and desire.

Matter: a sleep in which the dreamer dreams he is dreaming: a whorl of revolutions: currents, veils, recurrence,

where I is one alien: some thing else: which.

On the seabed, a form germinates, embedded, and wriggles free: a self-loosened creature cracks the shells from its back

and swims through the spectral currents, a cord among the tides, raising white clouds of names, writing, rewriting the sands,

dreaming it is dreaming, a being being dreamed. And a mouth breaks the meniscus: organs sense above

an unhorizoned air it cannot breathe but choke in, margins unimagined, a scope of music and rainbows,

and the dream it turns and returns in, is an allegory of that waking: a shard to throw away, a maze to recover that target through, a wreath composed of its absences.

The moment's thin surface, taut and unplayed, splits open,

and I is its cry I am at the point it shatters the surface.

Time: a sleep in which the dreamer dreams he is waking.

History: this nightmare: whirlpool, vortex, maelstrom,

crystallising, dissolving, spawning and burying signs, depositing languages, silting word on word,

drowning god on god, eroding bone and stone, engulfing each moment with mirages, muffling its music with echoes:

matterings, murmurings, ripples among the senses; hidden tracks through them: glimpses, intimations;

and the time-borne creature is sentenced to its constant journeying between presences never arrived at:

to the dream murmuring deeper under the sleep of the moment, or the silence above its surface, the white dream of waking,

and both unattainable between these wavering margins: the source and target of saying mere pastness and futurition,

absences, abstractions, outlawed from the maze: the Word I am a hollowness: a remembrance, a desire,

and Man: the poet, the dreamer: this sleeping exiled creature.

To wake, to break the dream, to transgress its wavering margins,

to jump the brink between silences, to shatter its burden of gravities,

to breathe the unremembered atmospheres, to swim, to fly through its surface, to soar, to dive upwards,

to free the Word from its sentence in the womb of the moment,

to hatch out of broken time time's child, unconceived, unnamed,

an amphibian creature climbing out of history to conjugate the worlds,

this, the offence of poetry:

that white target of saying: the arc that blinded Homer, that presence of other silence that deafened Beethoven.

The half-fledged yawning creature abandons its watery nest. The bow that will fire it is stretched to the roots of time.

Given once beginningness, now is a creature living, a being I presupposed by death, by dreaming, dominated: given once beginningness,

now is its own transformation: a creature dying, a being I that dreams of waking in unbeginningness:

from the dreaming of its dying, the dying of its dreaming, through which and by which it is being dreamed and died,

from the passion of its passing, the passing of its passion, through which and by which it is being past and passed,

from the birth of its bearing and the bearing of its birth, through which and by which it is being born and borne

away from recursion towards its own self-naming,

waking, to say and call itself I am.

Then swarms of verbs: unnoted generations, creatures unknown, untamed by time, mood, voice,

unempowered powers, unimpaired by pairings, unimagined sharings, steps through unpaced dances,

by what feet to be measured, where, when to be begotten, foundling unnamed children, unentranced, unconceived,

undetermined presences, borne and yet unborn, unbeset as yet by the conditions of an I:

to hear your murmurings unsentenced, spores on wind unlanded, breaths unpunctuated,

now to draw you in, here, between these margins.

Thou, presence here/now: other half of I am that I am not:

thou, merely grazed, pure form. Thou, touched, crumbling, eroding. Embraced, thou melting, dissolving. I grasp again: vapour. Thou I clutch: nothing.

Smelt, thou, noon of flowering. Thou, inhaled again, rotted leaves. Inspired, thou smoke and embers. Thou I remember: exile.

Heard, thou inaudible music. Listened for again, an echo. Thou bird call I strain my ears for: only my own heart rattling. A drumbeat slow dying: thou, silence.

Thou, glimpsed, ring deep dazzling. Seen and confronted, thou blindness. I glance back, and peer into darkness. I stare ahead, still blackness. My craving eyes thou dizzied. I maddened for thou lost, where?

Thou, tasted, body bodiless. Swallowed, thou haleness, a hallowing. Digested, thou a hell: weariness, drunkenness. Thou, pissed and shat, hollowness. Inner famine and drought.

Thou, other half of I am that I am not, that these five senses cannot hold: presence ever and never, here, there, passing: passion now and now, and between them,

thou, otherness: absence where/when, half of I that I am not.

As thou I stammer spit me out, back in this sleep-drenched maze,

what are these droplets splintering, streaking away like fish? these silver arrows, shimmerings, reflections, slivers in shadow,

scatterings, recollections? meteors, spermatazoa? these spectres of a moment, specks of dust and ancestors,

seeds and ghosts of their promises, plankton of unplumbed languages,

unmeasured vibrations and echoings, these undeciphered babblings through oceans of air and gravities

sinking and swimming with, in, through me, and away? vanishings, apparitions, adrift between these margins,

untold generations that escape through nets of echoes,

always inaccurate aims, ineffectual soundings, creatures sentenced to drowning?

words, words, words. Now the target has grown invisible, the music has gone still:

their presence is out there motionless, the continuum seems unattainable, and the child down here, unborn: a remembrance, a desire.

Caught helpless under these waves, towards thou I am and away, under these moments' momentum, to and fro they swim,

among overhearings of bird call and glimpses of target and rainbow, but dispersed before and after, muffled, clouded, blurred.

And the accuracies of saying? here, where, gone. And the hearer, found, responding? there, an exile away.

And the mad eye of the fourth person singular in a fine frenzy rolling, loose between the margins,

and thou, its salt spilt, lost in a drop of the dream, these particles spun round on the backwash time drains from me,

and thou, its bitter residuum here I lap up, craving,

and thou, there drowning in languages, seed aswhirl on tongues,

dead, unborn, waiting: other: whither wilt thou fly?

Come, wake me from my senses, intruder I denied. Invader I betrayed, come heal and mend here, say. Unveil here and be danced, spore on wind unlanded, untamed generation:

thou, present even in absence, whose weight crushes my memory; thou, present only in absence, hammer that pounds my desire:

through these cracks and fissures in sleep, here between these
    margins,

be poured, and ground and grow, unconceived creature of time.

As the dream of now evaporates, dreaming I wake from now, in now do I wake, or dream I am awake?

To distinguish: birth from birth, and waking from waking:

that of a creature dying, and dying to sleep again, crying itself to dream it wakes into dreams of waking, and that irreversible journey out of learning and unlearning,

to the cry unuttered, none yet have uttered; that of revolutions, and that of an evolution;

the harsh cry of the mind turning back on itself, round, in, out of, over itself, to break apart its fetters by material hammers,

and the song of the mind superseding itself, firing, forging itself,

borne on an arc of words whose soaring and diving are one, to a target unbounded by gravities,

and the way an unremembering and an undesiring: in and out through these margins, an unbeginning.

Matterings, murmurings; glimpses, intimations:

I might learn from the ancient Hebrews, who considered themselves unworthy to pronounce the word or words: I am.

A Promethean offence to do so: Homer, blind; Tiresias, blind; Oedipus, blind.

Beethoven also, deaf: the madnesses of witnesses, their unnumbered wittering sacrifices, trances of awakening, their maimings and their martyrdoms:

each grain of their ash a seeding, a blueprint for seeing, a seedling: spores grounding and blossoming: a cup, a sword, a dance. Thou they buoy up, my other, shall not go under,

among such who guide like shamans throughout the conceived underworlds, who skim the waters like dragonflies,

who tread like water boatman, their passing an open secret through worlds born in worlds of the Word,

in and out through this dream, under these moments' momentum, to and fro, what moves:

this, the offence of poetry. Five senses is not (all) I am.

To conjugate the worlds between them, where between these margins, waiting,

borne in the wake of a dream, between moments and breaths, I listen.

Stumbling feet, spell it out: celebrate the worlds: conjugate that, that the constancy of presence is no beginningness.

The clumsiness of all this. My need for a new (or lost) language that can accommodate and deliver such 'thoughts' with ease:

a language of language: a cup, a sword, a dance. A language of languages: scope of music and rainbows: in which

the mad eye of the fourth person singular is not another thou or one to be won and lost, lost and won,

but the ground of I am; and in which to say

'He is the mad eye of the fourth person singular', is no spell to need decoding, presenting no dreams or desires, but spilling them into the continuum; and in which

this eye is I/thou is I am, conductor of rainbow and bird call,

and has no need to be mad or go blind, or to call itself mad or blind,

sleeptalking.

Much talk of decadence, of lostness of self and centre, of retreating to beginnings, of going back to advance:

but where? but when? All points are focus for presence. The dream: one, recursive, through generations of sleeptalkers, for every I that is.

Their alienation: one: from thou I am and am not. The Word ever escaping, between desire and remembrance, through the dissolving margins, alone, is unbearable exile.

But at this brink between silences, in the humming net of language, the centre is the threshold,

is the dissolving margins: the dream's meniscus breaks, and here/now is the saying, unveiling.

Then feet, go here only, go only to now: where/when else? One all ways I am.

Presence: an infinite constant, variably pouring, never exhausted, ever revelation:

how can I lose or be lost by that which I am is not? by that which is unfounded? by that which is unfound?

History: ground of presence, of that which I am is all ways.

In this untilled ground I am to find and found the worlds: this, the offence of poetry, to wake, to break the dream: to become the name Human.

Poetry: waking: through language, presence breaking, all eye, all I that is, all that I is and am:

about nothing: meaning: encompassing: transparency.

The poem: seeing; saying; through words, all worlds I am,

cradled between these margins, unremembering, undesiring:

each thing's threshold and centre: the spore unladen, landed:

thou, the ground and the grounding: thou, the foundling,

child of time conceived, born, rooting and routing the silences, named, crying I am, conjugating the Word.

The hearer, found, responds: a cup, a sword, a dance.

The white target takes shape out of the dissolving rainbow.

That other silence is emptied in the song I am.

We too are dissolved in transparency.

The Rose of Sharon

The fire, the fire is falling!

BLAKE

I

When primeval dusts were formed
and the stars sprayed on the skies
and the fallow clays were warmed
and grew temples, feathers, eyes,

O what shrinkage of his power,
through what waste and in what rages
were the seeds of my love's flower
scattered down deserted ages.

But what spores spread down the wind,
what sparks through the thunder break,
how he laughs, my love, to find
a word alive, a man awake.

II

Moses on the mountain saw
jewels blazing at his throat,
ornaments without a flaw
and upon the tablets wrote:

you who crown his loveliness,
spreading perfume round his name,
garment for his nakedness,
diadem around his flame;

generations of repose
veil you from his naked eye,
multifoliate thornless rose,
on your bed of ashes lie.

III

Heracleitus copied this
from the same text in the fire:
crucified on every kiss
charred by night in man's desire,

you who bore his burning oil
and were chalice for his sword,
chosen vessel for his foil
withered now, and self abhorred,

out of time your wedding glory
withered now and nearly dead,
who are but a children's story
buried in a madman's head.

IV

Now a cock in Hades crows
and the sleepy hooded owls
sicken as nights foetus grows:
adam kadmon, in their bowels.

Listen for the fire falling
from his breath in searing rain.
Ages thick with ghosts are wailing,
pour your fire through us again!

Jar of nights and jar of days,
cracked in time from end to end,
gather up these broken rays,
yoke and seal them, heal and mend!

Ys

Of the city of Ys, this is how it is: seven crystal walls of various colours surround it, the first and outermost wall being the highest, and the second inside that higher than the third, the third higher than the fourth, and so on, until the citadel is reached inside the seventh wall. The tops of all the walls reach to the same height, for the island slopes up out of the sea on a long gradual incline towards its centre, where the cathedral stands, its spire being the only feature within the entire city visible to the voyager who sees the place from a distance over the water, or on a clear day from the high jutting cape of the mainland, seven miles eastward. The first wall is of colourless coarse quartz and rises unevenly and vertically out of the granite rock-face to a height that appears stupendous to one immediately below it. On all sides the place is surrounded by the sea, which throws innumerable shimmerings, glitterings and shadows up on the wall's rough surface, breaking and refracting the light into every colour, texture and nuance imaginable, according to conditions of wind and weather and the quality and time of day and season; and like the sea itself watched from the side or stern of a tall ship, this light is never still, now shattering into countless stars, now cloudy or dark, now flecked with rainbows, now white as foam wake. And you may well consider how this place appears to an observer or traveller gradually approaching it by sea from the bay beyond the cape head, which is the only mode of access: how dazzling and aloof, like a rough broad pillar of fire or cloud, gigantic in its proportions, crowned by the thin spire pointing up like a needle of ice or sword-blade at the sky. The tide rises between sixteen and thirty feet and the city may be entered only at high tide, by a flood-gate cut into the rockwall ten feet or so above the low tide mark. The aperture is narrow, and permits only a small boat to pass through. Above the entrance is a portcullis which can be lowered in a moment and so render the island wholly impregnable. Within this lies the harbour, which is full of these small craft, most of them used for fishing but some for transporting merchandise and visitors to and from the mainland. The quayside is decked with banners throughout the year and the small stone houses, taverns, shops and warehouses that constitute the port of Ys are all painted over with a pale blue wash, except for the roofs which are of slate. In the daytime, until the wall casts its long forbidding shadow, the harbour echoes with shouts of playing children. To the west of the island, towards the grey expanse of the Atlantic, lies a broken line of jutting rocks that gradually diminish in size to a permanent ridge of a shelf that once projected above sea level. On the nearest and largest rock the remains of a slate-built chapel erode and disintegrate, but apart from this, the rocks house nothing. No birds nest there, for the wind is too strong, though gulls, terns and the occasional razorbill wheel around them, gliding on the wind currents, and sometimes settling there to pause between their fishing and their aerial play. Here the waters are dangerous but on the mainland side the currents are easily navigated by an expert steersman, except in winter and during storms.

So much for the outer aspect and sea wall. The second wall is of sapphire and is surrounded by beds of cornflowers, honesty, forget-me-nots, bluebells, love-in-the-mist and other such delicate flowers in their season, offset here and there by small clumps of tough prickly briar, which bear faint-smelling five-petalled pink dog roses throughout summer and scarlet hips in autumn. This wall varies between a dull olive at dawn, to peacock at noon, to blue-of-ink in the evening. Apart from the harbour area, the space between the first two walls is covered by open pasture where short-horned cattle, ponies and horses graze freely, interspersed with woods that contain a great variety of trees, some of them very old. The third wall is of emerald and is surrounded by a ring of coniferous trees, none of which grows to the full height of the wall though they have never been lopped or pruned. The fourth wall is of amethyst, and is surrounded by vines and fruit trees: plum, pear, apple, cherry and fig. These trees are ordered radially, as evenly spaced quincunxes, into seven groves which are divided by open paths of worn flagstones. The cattle, ponies and horses, as well as sheep, goats, pigs, and ducks, geese and chickens are quartered in rows of sloping wooden sheds along most of the inner circumference of the amethyst wall. The fifth wall is of jaspered opal, whose smooth texture clouds in places to a thin opacity, as of water laced unevenly with milk, but for the most part reveals the continuous flickering of thousands of minute, multi-coloured flowers breaking open and dissolving beneath its surface. Between this and the wall of amethyst lies a patchwork of small fields and strips of land divided by narrow dykes, which are never quite straight or symmetrical, marked at every dozen or so intersections by a water pump or well. Some of these are disused, others relied on daily, and a variety of crops is sown here. Inside the opal wall the houses of the city are first seen, and behind them the sixth wall, which is built of chalcedony, varying in colour between onyx, agate, cornelian, chrysoprase and sard. The houses here are low, of one or two storeys, with summer swallows nesting under their ivy-covered eaves, over narrow streets barely wide enough for two carts to pass each other, between thin strips of low-walled gardens in front and behind, containing carefully tended perennial flowers and shrubs well pruned. Beyond the sixth wall are many more buildings, somewhat higher than those outside it, and grander and more ornamental in design and architecture, particularly those which are public places. Some have spacious inner courtyards lined with porticos and fountains at their centres. Here eight broader streets, spaced radially at equal distances from one another, transverse three concentric avenues, the second of which is the busiest thoroughfare of the city. On the mainland side, this avenue opens into a large square full of covered market stalls and surrounded by shops, taverns, hostels, places of entertainment, and the senate, library and administrative buildings. The seventh wall is of adamant and within this stands the cathedral, with its towers, turrets and buttresses on all sides and its central spire.

So both the innermost and the outermost walls are of colourless crystal, which is not to say that they display no colours to the human eye, but like the fifth wall of jasper, in the first and seventh walls all colours may be seen, which is as it should be.

A vertical and direct ascent to the central point and apex of the city-island is impossible, nor may you traverse the entire diameter of any of the rings within the first five walls more than once, for each concentric wall is joined to the one within it by another high radial wall. These are cunningly built on the left hand side of each gate, so that you must walk the entire circumference of each ring before you come to the gate opening on to the next ring, until you reach the city itself. So the ascent involves right-turnings, and the descent left-turnings, which is as it should be, and the island is structured like the whorl of a shell or primeval sea-creature, cut open to the sky.

Under the city, spanning the island from east to west, it is said there is a tunnel flowing deep under sea level, although none that I know of has ever discovered its exact location. Some say this was excavated by the first heathen generations of settlers; others, that it was eroded by the sea itself since time immemorial. A related story has it that under the floor of the lowest and central vault of the present cathedral, immediately below the level of its first foundation stone, is buried the rim of a well, over five yards in diameter, precariously lined with spiral steps leading vertically down to this submarine tunnel, which was either built by one of the early rulers or perhaps hollowed out of some long defunct volcanic flue. Before reaching the tunnel, it is said this well opens into a vast-domed, alembic-shaped cavern, just above sea level, where the first kings of Ys kept their treasures and mined their forgotten ores. However, neither I nor so far as I know any inhabitants since written records were kept have been able to verify either of these stories or find the entrance to the stairway, and I dare say they are both unreliable as are many such legends.

Fragment, from the Welsh. Date and author uncertain.

Transformations

from Rimbaud's *Les Illuminations*

Quince: Bless thee, Bottom! bless thee! thou art translated. (*Exit.*)
Bottom: I see their knavery: this is to make an ass of me; to fright me, if they could. But I will not stir from this place, do what they can: I will walk up and down here, and I will sing, that they shall hear I am not afraid.

A Midsummer Night's Dream

In Memory of Frances Richards, Painter

Sullen gulf. Sudden silence. Frances is gone.
Twice my age, my contemporary,
I thought her unbreakable.

I'm tired, she said, but went on working
right to the end. She hummed old hymns
meanwhile, and themes from music hall.

Nobody will nurse me, she laughed. I won't
let them. Once that happens you might as well
give up for good. You just stop.

Her wit could etch a line through cliché
and ricochet off chit-chat like
a phrase of Sappho or Socrates.

She bossed and loved her daughters
who grew up, took no notice
and teased and loved her back as she deserved.

She adored her husband and made him. His fame
was in part the doing of her patience and
she outlived him fourteen years.

Her heart of Burslem, Clay Town,
did not collapse. She shunned hacks,
despised phoneys, liked children,

drank a bit, went quiet sometimes,
got depressed, then pulled herself up
to all five feet two of her genius.

Her laughter was more resilient,
supple, infectious, than anyone's.
It bounced higher, more alive.

She was tough, beautiful, always
courteous. Her work is spiritual
and belongs to the world. Celebrate her.

Dawn

Moony haired and mysterious Aurora,
while shadows camped in woods, how is it I,
yes I, once held you, swan-downed, in my arms?
summer. Time was still water. I walked away
waking winds and jewelled dews, while wings rose soundlessly.
    I woke you, Dawn, I held you in my arms
    before the cockerels stirred life from the farms.

on one light-splintered footpath, a bold flower
told me her name. By blonde pigtailed waterfalls,
threading through pines, I laughed. On, on, I climbed
to the summit, where I touched white morning's veils,
and, Apollonian, I lifted them, one by one.
    she fled me down the transepts of my heart,
    transparent, while I prised warm air apart.

Around city steeples, domes, on marble quaysides,
I chased, barefoot, in rags, like an untouchable,
I grabbed at her through laurel groves, by waysides,
panting, I tore at her veils, my poor beggar girl,
yet grazed only skin surface of her immensity.
    Dawn, with her child, fell in woodland, ruddy fingered.
    We woke at noon. They were gone. Her perfume lingered.

'Dawn' – Frances Richards

Awakening

A scent of female angels in this dawn
beckons me, half asleep, to mount their hill
whose green gilt daggers, pointed up at heaven,
accuse my burning nights of birth in hell.
Ah, but I've escaped now, safe with these wool-robed creatures.
    They flee from me who sometime did me seek
    for flame, I cannot move or think or speak.

Fire rises on my right from dream-torn battles,
but, look, how dawn progresses on my left.
My woolly angels bleat. Like whorled sea-conches
they moan and murmur, hurrying me aloft
out of reach of my feverish nightmare murderers.
    They mingle breeze, warmth, thyme and lanolin
    with vision, they leap into brain and skin.

Below, around, float soft abysmal stars,
pouring, as from a basket, overflowing,
invisible, as flakes of summer sunlight
or angels, now it is morning, petals flying,
as, down from my drowsy hill, I slide into daybreak.
    Abysmal angels, sacrificial sheep,
    protect me, I have woken from my sleep.

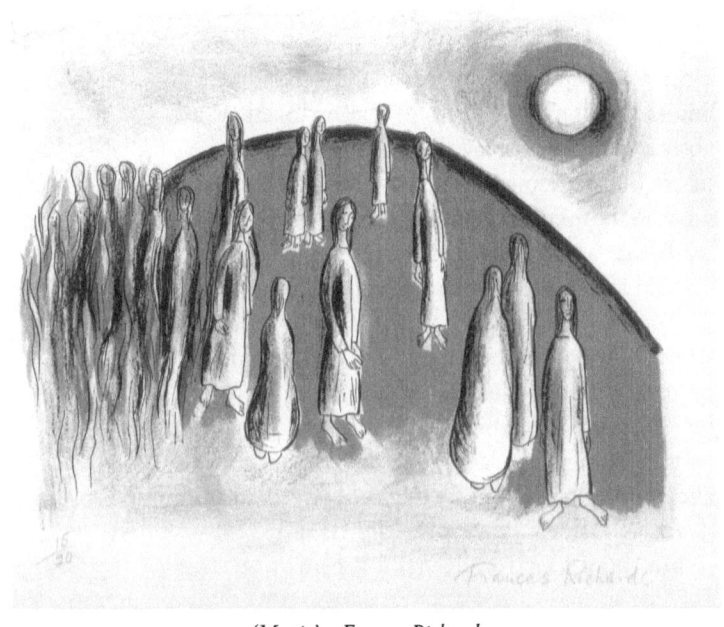

'Mystic' – Frances Richards

Midsummer

Under a greeny dawn, two naked women
embrace a donkey, three quiet heads together,
abstract, intent on play. Behind, a fourth
figure but half embodied, grows from the others,
whose face might be man's, faerie, or wingless angel.
    Is that an ass, or angel in disguise,
       and is this, perfect, dream or paradise?

Absurd, neck stretched, with one ear cocked,
quite still, the hooved ass sings, as if he knew,
by chorusing this dawn that peals and floods
its pale illuminated lake through greeny space
and sniffing grassy air, he might be loved all summer.
    An ass, asleep, how can I tell I dream
       but think I see I understand I seem?

He stands with forelegs hidden, lost in women,
entwining with them, naked, in peaceful glory,
So his head on a woman's frame I see
with centaur, tamed for human company,
in sexed or sexless union, summer, magical.
    What rules, when male or female centaur is
       alive and well, across the centuries?

Bottom – Frances Richards

Memory

Look, there's my alien childhood, ashen, cold,
sunk, dead now, lain behind that flowering rose,
and I, your mother, Memory, who've come down
and found you here, know now that no surprise
can shake me more, from this, my weariest of purposes.
    This white worn flight of steps I have descended
    was my life also. Here, my journey's ended.

My birth, your younger brother, waits below
the sunset, to be crushed. You I was, child,
our homes and haunts have been shut down, and chilled
swarms of dead bees piled high around them. Walls
block all inside but tops of trees, too high for insight.
    Their keys have been thrown away, because we've died.
    Anyway, nothing exists to see inside.

Look, the field slopes golden to the villages,
the lock gates open, buzzing rainbow hives
sail past haystacks, and windmills chime on wind,
stopping time on their calvaries. Hay, hooves
of flowers and fabled beasts once quietly drummed that hillside.
    Over seas – eternities of hot tears,
    cloud masses groaned afar, and meshed in years.

'Childhood II' – *Frances Richards*

Two Lakes

Two lakes, joined,
one above the other
along the same river:

Upstream, the Derwent
and, below,
the Ladybower.

When two lakes join
together they
do not dry up.

One draws the other
through constant
self-replenishing.

Upstream, the Derwent
and, below
the Ladybower.

Joyousness:
two lakes, joined,
one above the other.

Tree

*The tree of life groweth with slow and
steady increase through unmeasured time*

BASILIDES OF ALEXANDRIA

Tree planted
  in my core
spreading growing
  tree of songs
many branched
  flame tree
rooted in death
  blood bathed
breath blown
  bone fibred
body tree
  elemental
tree in a seed
  full throated
thousand tongued
  thick skinned
creaking tree
  enduring thunder
wind eroded
  snow bound
survivor tree
  skeletal
under storm clouds
  budding slow
through despair
  thrusting hopes
of high skies
  cirrus strewn

milky ways
   and birds returning
wakening
   sleep laden tree
circled in memories
   close grained
springwood
   and summerwood
tree of dreams
   and visitations
leaved with hair
   of fallen heroes
snake wreathed
   giant guarded
threaded with voices
   and children's laughter
ancestor tree
   earth drinking
sky swallowing
   bowelled living
grave tree
   light eating
pillar of wisdom
   of smoke of cloud
desert beacon
   whorled tornado
fire fountain
   golden chain
leading the way
   through night
with agate jet
   and haematite

from evening
  gathering emerald
carnelian
  and diamond dews
and in the studded
  bowl of dawn
with pearl and opal
  dissolving them
spreadeagled
  against the morning
a scented trellis
  spanning noon
blue crowned
  tree of earth
water fire
  of air of airs
light ship
  dusky barge
sailing on
  wind seasoned
around year ends
  and back again
clay moored
  soil harboured tree
prow lapped
  by heaven's tides
sun cradle
  moon basket
cloud blanketed
  cask of stars
rocking meteors
  shaking planets

ploughing galaxies
  on long oars
world hammering
  sky raking
word breaking
  rocksplitting tree
bonecracking
  wrist of boughs
tower of strength
  pivot fulcrum
axial roof tree
  probing pharos
ever turning
  clawed through crust
of cliff and crag
  pointed dactyl
spark igniting
  flame hurling
quill clutched
  in a stone fist
illuminating
  day's page
in green and gold leaf
  manuscript
chiselling plaques
  in night's crypt
with serifs inked
  in baryons
kindling speech
  of origins
to sing darkness's
  molten core

of ice
   moss and coal
fossil fern
   and dinosaur
time tree
   revolving burning
prising open
   history's lips
drilling its jaws
   to spit pips
needle twigs
   and wiry shoots
earthed in its seams
   and blood routes
ore flowers
   on brittle stems
magnetic amber
   diadems
electric tree
   lightning conductor
energy funnel
   through stratospheres
chimney built
   in the pot of death
fuelling years
   with quiet breath
tree of creation
   tree of destruction
temple planted
   in an upturned skull
worming woody
   fibres through

eye socket
   and mandible
world tree
   scroll keeping
cave covered
   by sky mountain
joy tent pitched
   in wilderness
dome whispering
   spire trembling
gargoyle gnarled
   buttress of hills
glory cone
   mist piercing
latticed steeple
   nesting angels
fan vaulted
   echoing tree
runged ladder
   for the soul's fingers
valved throat
   winged glottis
ringing singing
   ribcage tree
harmonising
   forest airs
and air of plains
   in symphony
with the unceasing
   ocean feud
orchestral baton
   dowser's rod

dipping bending
   greenwood sapling
bowed by longing
   flex of hope
tightrope stretched
   from loam to God
tuned wand
   alembic
caduceus twined
   branching vessel
thermometer measuring
   ages' heat
mercurial sap
   rising falling
hollow tree
   fluted with stomata
wooden well
   mine tunnelled
bell cord
   and lungs of Hades
gale harness
   fanning the damned
and the twice dead
   and the never born
with harp tinkling
   in glen and glade
and lament of orchards
   for Hesperides
womb tree
   moist lipped
rain collecting
   underground tree

resin caulked
  wine vat
tree of desire
  taboo fruited
mountain spring
  orgy scented
waterfall
  weeping tree
flooded river
  magma breasted
lava tree
  sowing islands
eddying delta
  coral tree
perpetually blazing
  deciduous
tree of madness
  tree of passion
set with thorns
  sweating blood
pain tree
  evergreen
showering ghosts
  shedding children
common tree
  brittle old
crowded stunted
  overshadowed tree
insect gnawed
  rot infected
lightning blasted
  husk of famine

raped mutilated
   people's tree
obelisk
   dead tree
uprooted felled
   sawn plank
hearth tree
   for warmth and fuel
table tree
   for bread and wine
architraved
   thyrsus totem
bound and staked
   earthed and fused
blood spattered
   royal trunk
nailing hell
   to paradise
gallows tree
   rising again
knuckled knotted
   blind man's staff
swordblade
   heavy hilted
thick boled
   ivory tusk
ebony spear
   erect conquering
tree in a prairie
   in a city garden
pruned and tended
   by patient hands

quiet tree
  of yes of no
of this of that
  of black of white
confluence
  of pasts and futures
rooted in ever
  praising now
flesh tree
  rimmed in muscle
blood and sweat
  sighing shivering
shuddering tree
  generous
sperm tree
  life pump
ever brimming
  around whose roots
the serpent coils
  around whose branches
flits the white bird
  tree of spirits
tree of secrets
  buried in heaven
to flower through veins
  arteries nerves
capillary tree
  meristematic
your tap root drowned
  in infinite skies
I descend up
  and ascend down

rod of aeons
   of Adam Kadmon
Jesse David
   and Sataniel
and Moses
   on the high mountain
Buddha tree
   Tilopa tree
zen tree
   tantric tree
Kali's tree
   dancing on skulls
volcanic tree
   of Ashtaroth
Lilith
   Ishtar and Astarte
nurturing
   moss and lichen
mould gathering
   mushroom tree
mother of orchids
   and mistletoe
tree of Dryads
   tree of Druids
where the spider weaves
   and the rooks nest
and the bat flitters
   and the kestrel waits
tree of lives
   of consciousness
generative
   language tree

speaking names
   telling stories
histories
   transformations
depthless tree
   deathless tree
tree of comrades
   of airs I breathe
unpruned
   untameable
immortal tree
   overarching
freedom tree
   tree of love
tree of justice
   human rainbow
blossoming

Day Estate

Here is a harsh and bitter cry.
                    ABEL MEEROPOL

Matins

Dawn. The wind wipes off the river's
slick meniscus and drops it here
behind the pylons and the docks
to congeal, freeze, solidify.
It smothers slates and chimney stacks
like a huge tear-stained handkerchief.
This city, like a bleary eye
stung by it, blinks and quivers.

Then you can almost smell the fear
seep out of the bricks and stones
and gather strength like a ghost
to split, clone, multiply.
In every haunted face it locks
lips and jaws. It squats and groans.
It rattles like a poltergeist
in tenement dwellers' homes.

Oppression, doubly-bonded glue,
pastes estates and tower blocks
in closely knit communities
for everybody knows this is
not curable by tax relief
or extra Christmas bonuses.
To take whatever they can give us
and cringe, *More please?* Lord. Forgive us.

Lauds

As dreams dispersed by consciousness
dissolve on light-crests and recede,
gassed in their mental furnaces,
beyond recall, out of control –
their questions all gone answerless
(*What has happened to your soul?*) –
in lieu of sunrise, a sulphurous
sky bleeds yellow over us.

Dawn, but no sunrise. The sun falls
up – slides – hides – uncertain
whether to hang dissolved in mist
like a faint sheen, half suspended,
or, filtering through net and curtain
and tossing shadows on damp walls,
peer around frayed dreams, unended,
and prod us awake to – rise? resist?

Light lurks, like an attendant nurse
outside a ward where someone's crying,
tactful, very quiet, of course,
and too bad if the patient's dying.
While night, with all its phantoms, palls,
a waking nightmare shrouds and shawls
day in its drab materials.
Morgues batten fast on hospitals.

Lord's Prayer

Arise, my Love, and greet the morning.
But why rise if you're on the dole?
Better practise subtle patience
and exercise a strict control
on appetite, on energies –
for here's our bailiff on patrol
delivering fresh anxieties
with yet another Latest Warning.

There's someone leaning on the bell
who won't take No, and go. The Creep.
So get you up and out of bed.
Wrapped up but shivering, half asleep,
unshaven, skinny, limbs like lead,
tottering, barely vertical,
rip wide open the demands
on bills unpaid, unpayable.

Now come on Mister, please. No fuss.
All right mate. I'm not deaf or dead
but Master of this Citadel
even though disinherited.
It's rough on you and tough on us.
We can't wait, see. Oh Jesus, will
no House of Commons succour us?
Nor House of Lords? Lord, suffer us.

Antiphons

Wake up my love and light the fire.
I can't. We've got no wood or coal.
*Then get yourself down to the store
and buy some, will you?* What with, girl?
You must be joking. No I'm not.
The last two bags we had, I stole.
Look in my purse. See what I've got.
Oh just wrap up. *I hate this hole.*

Now tenements, like coffin lids,
in long bleak gloomy ranks, upended,
yield up their sullen occupants,
the living dead, upon the morning.
as if fixed in some ghastly dance
from which all zest has been suspended,
we cross the waste where someone's kids
mine? yours, maybe? play unattended.

Wrap up. *It's cold, love.* Walk slow. Stroll
drab streets, mix with the silent crowd,
join queues for jobs where worker ants
sign on in airless offices,
haggle for extra supplements
from sour deliverers of our dole,
for everybody knows this is
where we wrap up in morning's shroud.

Common Octaves

Hi. I'm Gargoyle and my hair's green.
I'm a Grass Grower. See what I mean?
And she's Prudence and her hair's pink.
She don't give a toss what you think.
Him there? That's Muskrat, with the Mohican.
Sometimes he's sane, sometimes freaking.
And him, Spiderman, he's my mate.
You was born too early and him too late.

And that high jumper, that's Billie the Kid.
His take home pay is two hundred quid.
That's for sixty nine hours a week.
Work that one out before you speak.
If you ask me – or Billie here – or Muskrat –
freaking is what we're specialist at.
And puking and belching
and tossing and squelching.

Whatever architect designed
this place must have had in mind
some ghastly cornerstone of Hell,
even Hell's inner citadel.
Heeow Neeow, he never. What he thought of
wasn't really what he ought of.
Not trash. Not us. Being posh
He was after Clout, see, Charles. And Dosh.

Sexts: Unpunctuated Anthem

A leader for our pains
surgeon of our national
wealth and hellfire system
saint of broken promises
and underwriter of soul
drainage programmes

Investor in normal lies
shareholder in triplethink
honesty detector
demagogue of imperious
and loudmouth cliché
backed by troupes of connivers

Top agent and representative
for internal hope-manipulation
and aspiration processors
poverty provider
leecher of wages
planned dole director

Careful energy squanderer
and armoured glory baron
smartclad in hack moralities
rank organiser of street
cosh and carry shielded
uniformed gang bully boys

Prison prescribing guardian
of short sharp hypocrisies
mind misery minister
home cancer producer
grin carver and overall
comptroller of orphanages

Smallholder of twisted empire
land and sea overdrafter
cool polluter of heavens
pension thief hunger breeder
bombhoarder soulmonger sharp
eyed state roulette racketeer

SUFFRAGE

*The best use for a safety pin
is to tie up Liberty in.
The best way to use good thick rope
is strangle God. Until there's hope.
The best thing to do with your fists
is clench them tight. Till Love exists.
The best knuckle duster's a blue tattoo
spelling* LOVE *to us,* HATE *to you.*

*Now what you do with a Union Jack
is hang it from your belt, front to back,
down purple jeans with green spots.
That tells the Haves from the Have-Nots.
And that's only part of the gear.
The rest? Dole. Dope. Fags. Fear.
If that's funny, we ain't even started.
We wasn't born when God farted.*

*What else do you expect in Great Britain?
Love it? Like hell. But we don't fit in.
Sure we're scum, slime, filth, detritus.
So call more coppers out to fight us,
Bring out the army and the tanks.
Really charmed to be interviewed.
Shall we do it again, Charles, nude?
Suck you mate. Who needs your thanks.*

Angelical Salutations

Are you empty yet? An angel just passed by.
His speckled wings were twinkling against the evening sky.
He was looking for applicants. So why don't you apply.
Oh now, I see you think you might have time to cry,
because it's all too much, isn't it, not understanding why.
So why not have the courage, friend? It won't hurt you to try
to be a little emptied, a little emptied before you die.

Mother, Mother, the images are longing for your breast.
They're lining up outside the door along with all the rest.
They're queuing up for tickets, waiting to get undressed.
They don't know that you're occupied already with a guest,
and if they did know, Lady, I doubt they'd be impressed.
This is no time for slumbering, or numbering the blessed.
Do you reckon all the things you've done can ever be confessed?

Are you empty yet? An angel just passed by. (etc.)

Look, nobody who lives round here knows what it's all about.
The only thing we know round here is our one religion – Doubt.
And we haven't got the energy, or genius, or clout,
Or willingness, or interest. They've all gone up the spout.
That bloke you thought was an angel must've been some layabout.
Look, if you want a ticket, mate, ask any friendly tout,
And if you catch sight of an angel, kick the bastard out.

Are you empty yet? An angel just passed by. (etc.)

Nones

Pearly twilight. Freezing fog's
orphan fingers wipe the phlegm
from the rags of a February day,
smearing it in uniform
grey stains on walls and windows
no police or policies
will patch up or wipe away.

Come in, duck. Would you like a cuppa
here where damp soaks our little room?
We're sorry you can't stay for supper
in our friendly family tomb,
Yes, everybody knows it's not
going to improve a lot,
and yes, we're sorry that you find us
living so, but be so kind as

to send somebody that don't mind us –
no nice well-meaning councillors
who really care, and serve as pillars
of hack and half-plastered reform.
Come strike and protest, wind and storm –
Everybody knows this is
where you get put, and you stay
and lump it. Or go to the dogs.

Evensong

Dusk's revelations. Half wild curs
are let out, starving, masterless,
to race dark over the Estate,
night rangers, rabid harbingers.
On concrete slabs torn up and scattered
from alleyway and underpass,
on cracked tarmac, they snarl and mate
and howl down streets. As if it mattered.

Now come on, stroll out. Flex some muscle
up at the corner of the grid.
That rumble? Just a passing train?
That rattle? Just a dustbin lid?
Two kids engage. Bit of a tussle?
Somebody's down. Somebody lugs
some body off, makes sure it's hid.
The lads collect again to jostle.

A prowl car stabs the evening wide.
Headlamps dip the street in mustard.
Make way. Blue flashing. Cops again.
What's going on? Now don't get flustered.
He's pissed mate. He don't feel no pain.
A drunk leans out, screams, *Suicide.*
Och leave the puir wee bairns alane.
And shrieks, *Ye fascist copper bastards.*

COMPLINE

Go home. Past wall signs on the stairs
predicting or invoking chaos,
stinking of brimful trash-cans, beer,
cat musk and ashes, urine, dung,
Crack Rules OK (if so, who cares),
up five long flights, hope no-one stirs,
and hope no heavies will waylay us –
Make way. Go home. Where dad will slay us.

Make way. the British night is young
for slum dwellers and unemployed
and beggars dossing in the park
beneath the system's lowest rung.
The Ministry's Behind the Void.
Our Shareholders invest in Fear.
The Government supports the Dark.
Who needs a Revolution here?

Is that a song? Or wind? Make way.
Make way for the approaching storm.
Pin hopes on now, not yesterday.
Rip off the patchwork of reform –
where we, mere exploitation's mugs,
cringe, curl and wag our tails, like curs.
Make way for justice, ruling thugs.
Make way, law-licensed murderers.

Whose shuffle is that? On the stair?
He's been snorting smack. Or underwear.
Ride a cock horse to Holy Cross.
The horse is night. He's a dead loss.
Time for a game? *Stone scissors paper.*
Stoned? Go on, you try and wake her.
You win, Death. *Scissors paper stone.*
When you die die you die alone.

Make haste to town, Lord, make haste.
Everything here's a cheat or waste.
Thing is, Eh-Knee-Arse, she's O-deed.
Oh dear oh Dido that's all we need.
For a slice of peacock pie in the sky
That ain't no reasonable way to die.
Hush little baby, won't you sleep.
Easy come. Easy go. Dirt cheap.

Vigil: Privileged Octaves

Across the mud, across the river,
someone is playing Lady Day
on a portable cassette deck
and that cracked voice, of lead and silver,
is mirroring – all – I – wish – I – could say.
*You make me feel – so sad. You make me
think of all the things I never had –*
is about blowing myself all away.

Carry me, wind, that voice of human
suffering in stereo.
Bring her – her – *glory?* – back tomorrow.
Bring – her back – *all-of-her* – here, today:
hope out of heartache, brave broken woman,
hope things'll change here (some day they may),
hope come shivering naked from horror
warmed in a small patch of sun.

Hope is not vanity, calleth the preacher.
Hope is truth's fountain, whispereth the stream,
*hope is no weakened mind's pretty picture
afloat on some fool's or fantasist's dream.*
Hope, saith the breeze, *blows through each creature.*
Hope bears truth, love and justice for theme . . .
You make me feel – so sad. You just make
me wish my wish for hope could reach her.

Black Light

In memory of George Seferis, 1900–1971

... What matters above all is the quality of the light. Not only in the cloudless days of summer but even in winter the light is unlike that of any other European country, brighter, cleaner and stronger. It sharpens the edges of the mountains against the sky, as they rise from valleys or sea; it gives an ever-changing design to the folds and hollows as the shadows shift on or off them; it turns the sea to opal at dawn, to sapphire at midday, and in succession to gold, silver, and lead before nightfall; it outlines the dark green of the olive-trees in contrast to the rust or ochre soil, it starts innumerable variations of colour and shape in unhewn rock and hewn stonework. The beauty of the Greek landscape depends primarily on the light, and this had a powerful influence on the Greek vision of the world.

C. M. BOWRA, *The Greek Experience*

There is a drama of blood played out between the light and the sea, all around us here, that very few sense. It is not sensualism; it is something much deeper than the fleeting desire and the so persistent smell, let's say, of woman that prisoners yearn for. There is a drama of blood much deeper, much more organic (body and soul), which may become apparent to whoever perceives that behind the grey and golden weft of the Attic summer exists a frightful black; that we are all of us the playthings of this black. The stories we read about the houses of Atreids or Labdacids show in some way what I feel. Attic tragedy, the highest poetic image of this hemmed-in world, constantly striving to live and breathe upon this narrow golden strip of land, meanwhile, with little hope of being saved from sinking to the bottom. This creates its humaneness.

GEORGE SEFERIS, *Journal*, 17 JUNE 1946

Light, angelic and black
laughter of waves on the sea's highways,
tear-stained laughter,
the old supplicant sees you
as he moves to cross the invisible fields –
light mirrored in his blood,
the blood that gave birth to Eteocles and Polynices.
Day, angelic and black;
the brackish taste of woman that poisons the prisoner
emerges from the wave a cool branch adorned with drops.
Sing little Antigone, sing, O sing . . .
I'm not speaking to you about things past, I'm speaking about love
decorate your hair with the sun's thorns,
dark girl;
the heart of the Scorpion has set,
the tyrant in man has fled,
(land all the daughters of the sea, Nereids, Graeae,
hurry towards the shimmering of the rising goddess:
Whoever has never loved will love,
in the light:
          and you find yourself
in a large house with many windows open
running from room to room, not knowing from where to look out first,
because the pine trees will vanish, and the mirrored mountains,
     and the chirping of birds
the sea will drain dry, shattered glass, from north to south
your eyes will empty of daylight
the way the cicadas suddenly, all together, fall silent.

                George Seferis, from *Thrush*, 31 October 1946

In Memory of George Seferis (I)

Angelic and black, light . . .
Angelic and black, day . . .

Black is the light behind the blaze of day,
your summons comes, clear from the angel's throat.
The sun's black horses call your heart away.

Though bright the stain of dawn upon the bay
which in celestial ink its author wrote,
black is the light behind the blaze of day.

Though morning's cloudy mares are dappled grey
with rainbow mane and many coloured coat,
the sun's dark horses call your heart away.

Their riders gallop by. Too swiftly they
will trample down the shades noon kept afloat.
Black is the light behind the blaze of day.

Night's chariot approaches, Don't delay.
Haul evenings golden gate up. Cross the moat.
The sun's dark horses call your heart away.

You scent that whinnying wind? The horses neigh.
You see it now? You hear that perfect note?
Black is the light behind the blaze of day.
The sun's dark horses call your heart away.

The Voice

It's just the light . . . shadows of the night.

What is that voice from Hades down the street,
wafting up through a basement on the chords
of a baghlamá or bouzoúki plucked by racing fingers,
singing into the sunset and the tide,
ferreting my tribes of sadness from their warrens
beneath the cliffs this house of words is built upon?
It laps the bay. It flecks the evening light
with arrows that splinter the water, little needles
that prick my throat and sting my eyes with salt,
as though your beauty, world, would go on forever
unravelling from horizon to horizon,
not stitching itself along this hem of pain
consciousness wears brocaded in all its garments
against oncoming night, sleep, dream and death.
Tell me what is that voice that saps my breath
out of my body like a thirsty nomad
hauled over sand dunes by the scent of waters,
arriving at the Euphrates, and plunging his face in?

Soulmonger

How softly flowed the Thames among the shadows . . . Sleep well.

And my guide said, 'Do not probe too deeply in darkness
but construct your world out of daylight. As for dreams,
you should listen to them carefully, for their voices
may often be prophetic, pointing the true way
or, at least, contain some seed of unexpected wisdom
however uncertain and inchoate in form.
But since an honest mind's work is best done by day,
and 'Light' has always been a metaphor for 'Goodness',
and the spirit's true goal is communion with God,
never blindly follow a voice out of a dream;
rather train your mind patiently to hatch your soul,
a task which requires sorting carefully between
true counsellors, who may visit even at night,
and the false guides, tempters and ghostly apparitions
who will fasten your fledgling soul ever more firmly
to matter, the corrupt world of the ten thousand things,
which, you know, is illusion. For these are the Qelippoth,
against whom all our Qabalistic Masters warn us,
who, once your soul is weakened by constant forays,
may poison it utterly and gain complete sway,
thus disabling it from soaring ever again.
Remember the soul's wings are fragile as an insect's
and may be withered by excess of light, or darkness.
Above all, beware of conflicting daimons
who may tear a man to pieces: think of poor Rimbaud,
or Nietzsche who, in madness, signed himself Dionysos,
because he had dared penetrate the forbidden realm
of the Mothers. He would have been wiser to follow

Goethe's quiet path to knowledge, or the cooler
logic of Wittgenstein: Of that whereof one may not speak
it behoves to stay silent . . . Beware the black light.'

Half Celt, half Saxon, his blue flecked irises gleamed
as he lit a cigarette and poured me more whisky
across the table in his Notting Hill flat
strewn with books everywhere: my goodhearted old teacher,
a man in love with wisdom yet not greatly wise,
who first had brought me to Plato and Heracleitus
and read me from Homer in his Oxford Greek accent.
and this his gentle English way of saying Goodbye.
'Beware the black light,' he repeated as I left
and he closed his door behind me at 3 a.m.,
and I tottered down dark stairs into Linden Gardens
and walked, half drunk, through the winter night to Fulham.

Volta

. . . now that dusk falls . . .

King sun, rosy cheeked, day's sovereign coin,
you touch me, and my skin becomes a cornea,
my spine an optic nerve, and my body trembles
half dazzled by the pool of gold you pour
over this sea and city, and I'm blinded.
Here once stood rows – and still I know they stand –
of houses and streets, belonging to another city,
not this one you have utterly transformed.

We walk along the waterfront. The night
fishermen's boats are ready to set out,
motors chugging, paraffin lamps in the bows,
and the whole town's out for the promenade,
lovers arm in arm, and young men swaggering,
mothers and fathers, children eating ice-cream,
old men watching from tables at pavement cafés,
and the darkening hills move closer, like friendly animals.

Sweet evening skyglow, spread on hills and bay,
your arm grazes mine now, as if by accident,
like the touch of this young woman who walks beside me
with heavy hips, small steps and swinging gait,
jet hair swept back, delicate throat and shoulders
deep summer bronzed, and her olive brown eyes laughing.
I drink you, shimmering light, like wine, like music,
as her ancestors have drunk you thousands of years.

Porous city, her name is *Eleftheria*,
and though your scars are grey flecks in her eyes,
still, at this hour when light and light's inflections
play subtly in her face as speech or song,
hers is the ancient right to walk this quayside
as instrument and guardian of your light
collecting it in the wells of her deep pupils,
and hers, the darling freedom, to tread you like a dancer.

Darling evening, light thousands of years old,
clear throated singer, lovely as this woman,
how can I not adore the grace you cast
this city and its people in, a mould
that sculptures all it touches, the whole world?
I have become your slave, if not your citizen.
And thirsting to drink you wholly, I would fill
every pore with your radiance, her freedom.

Cicadas (I)

Once in Pelion I heard them
swiftly digging a cave
into the night

The men play *távli* and drink *tsípouro* or coffee,
skéto, metrio, glykí vrastó. Above our heads
the *nichterídhes* flitter among the plane trees
and every table but mine in the square is full.
Through voices thrum, laughter, clatter of board
and counter, clink of glasses, and fork against plate,
where the bald, bullied waiter runs, scurrying, sweating,
tonight I sit alone, trying to write a letter
home to my son and daughter: *Dearest Children* . . .

And furious, monotonous, insistent, oppressive,
all around, the cicadas beat on my ear drums.
Already their armies have marched out of the hills
down to the square's edge, and they have us under siege,
ready to invade, lying in wait below windows,
behind shrubs, in courtyards, and among flowering gardens,
and we are all hostages to these gentle barbarians
who press in, roaring, like waves of an inland sea.

They are hollowing a cave out of these night covered hills
and they will hole us up in it, until we drown in darkness.

Only the Common Miracle

. . . between your face and your face . . .

It isn't much to ask, only the common miracle, in the silent
    speech of lovers, the way I want to talk
to you, and you to me, is only a small sight away from angelic
    voices pouring out of blue skies without a single cloud
when you turn round and wonder who spoke to you but no-
    body's there
except on your left the same dusty track and the dry grass with the
    single fig tree in the field
and beyond its stone walls, the mountain, and on your right,
    the sea;

or when you stand astonished, in a street in some foreign city,
    thinking you heard a friend
greet you in your own language, someone very familiar once,
    you haven't seen for years
with the same old voice, laughing, playful, perhaps even slightly
    ironic,
and everything you had forgotten suddenly clears before you in
    the naked morning light, as the blood rushes to your head
and you forget your errand, the traffic stops, and the buildings
    start whirling about you;

or when, at passion's crest you open your eyes a moment to keep
    resurrection at bay
and between the face of the person you love and the face of the
    person you love
another face appears on the wave you've never seen before but
    always have known and will know
and a gap opens for a voice, which isn't yours or mine, but we
    both hear quite clearly, and recognise,
and understand, and adore, because you know as well as I do, my
    love, that it's your voice, not mine;

it's not much to ask, only the common miracle, but people like
    you and me have been travelling
like this for years, along the same dirt track through the same
    city streets the same weary beds
foreign in our own country, no longer recognising the speech of
    men or women we know, of our own flesh,
so how then can we be expected to converse with angels or even
    with old friends, long dead,
let alone speak the language of love, let alone the language of
    love?

SALT

laughter of waves on the highways of the sea

All I know is, friend, we're on our way to an island, with the sun
    above us scattering
opals on the morning, and our wake the folds of a robe draped
    on a *kóre*'s belly,
volcanic, liquefied stone, as if the statues marble body were
    dancing,
and Costas there at the tiller, who knows this sea, and keeps
    putting on cassettes of old songs,
and the rest of us drunk already, half on wine, half on sunlight,
    and singing.

Basking in this light that peals out of the sky, and leaps back
    echoing from everything it touches,
I don't want to chart our route, we're in safe hands, and there's
    no special hurry,
with these brown, sweat-scented girls on deck baring their
    breasts and laughing
a secret laughter, that makes them inviolable marble, the sea's
    own dancing daughters, and even when you graze
their clammy, oil-skinned arms, not naked in their nakedness,
    but clothed in the robes of the sun;

while for us, men, trapped in another kind of salt, there is always
 that other woman
who lies above us, invulnerable, regal in her indolence, her long
 legs enclosing an arc of the bay,
as she dozes on her right side, colossal in the sun, swathed in her
 own smell of orchards, goats and resin –
if I stretched out my arms I could almost touch her face, feel her
 cool fingers press into my shoulders –
but even with eyes closed, soft moaning in this sea breeze, she
 would still remain aloof, with that secret mountain smile.

By noon we'll have reached our island and moored at a quiet
 inlet, where we'll swim and scratch wet sand
and watch the little clams come out, almost eager to die for us,
 and gather them in hundreds and take them back on board,
then coast around to the harbour with no electricity, to feast by
 the quay on *kakaviás* and wine,
and a fisherman scraping a mussel half a metre long will give me
 its twin shells, hinges to open the sea,
and at sundown we'll start our engine and head back for the main-
 land, arms enclosing the shoulders of our tipsy, shivering
 girls.

So no charts, friend, this exacting light defeats them, just as the
    waves cancel our wake:
we're on our way to an island, and all I know is, I'm helplessly in
    love with this mountain and this sea,
for here desire and fulfilment are stitched in one weft of light,
    cross-woven, stilled and impossible to unravel
from this seamless tide of days which flow in one movement
    together, its whole fabric soaked and doubly strengthened
    in salt,
and mine is its crusted harvest with the perfect inner sheen, although I have gnawed summer down to its black core.

Neolithic

I'm not speaking to you about past things, I'm speaking about love.

Dark the plain, empty, waiting for summer rain. You had climbed
    the old citadel and were stumbling among the ruins
bruising your feet against half-buried walls, your legs grazed by
    nettles and thistles,
and the mountain, far to your right, asleep in the gloom like a
    dinosaur with ridges on its back
and the sea below scarcely visible, only a mile away, and insects
    bombarding your forehead
in the electric air, and your throat and lips parched as the sandy
    soil.

Once a lizard crossed your track and slithered away in dust, and
    once you saw a tortoise lumber through withering grass
as, below the kiln, disused four thousand years, you stooped to
    pick up shards, trying to fit fragments together,
or, overturning rubble, scratched neolithic grain, black as charred
    match-heads, which you crumbled between thumb and
    forefinger;
nothing cohered, and you lifted your head suddenly, thinking
    you heard a mule bray or smelt goats on the downwind
when, against the sky above you, you saw the old man standing,
    the skinny dog at his side, and you stood to greet him.

'Listen now,' his voice quiet, fingers clutching your right arm
    refusing to let it go,
'They won't let me stay much longer. They're calling me back with
    them to the other shore we came from
behind the blue island on the far side of this mountain. Listen
    to me carefully. There isn't much time.
All my life I hungered for this mountain, this sea, these islands,
    and although I moved among them
and my body was of their substance, stone, clay and brine, my
    hunger could not be sated if I lived ten thousand years.

'And now it is nearly finished, one thing I know: the black light
    is radiant
and is not to be feared. For if you look through, not at it, and see
    through unshadowed eyes,
you may know it also in daylight. For it is not merely blood,' he
    whispered, 'nor passion of the body,'
now grasping your arm more tightly, and the dark pools of his
    pupils blazed like twin suns in eclipse,
the irises surrounding them insufferably bright, and his harsh cry
    echoing across the valley:

'Blood, but not just blood. Passion, but not just of flesh. Whoever calls this foul is a liar or a fool
and will drown in his own lusts, however spotless his thought,
and only his bones be purified, like dead coral in sea caves,
for stone, clay, brine are particles of radiance. Light is mirrored in blood,
and those who love light as I do, know dark and light are one.
Hurry now, tell the children. There is not much time.
I'm not speaking to you about past things, I'm speaking about love . . .'

And he released your arm, turned, and strode through the rubble, gigantic,
and his dog whimpered, sniffed the air, and followed him up the hillside,
and you stood and watched them climb, till their shapes, like crumbling statues,
blurred into the rock-face, and thunder rang from the mountain
and rain poured on hills and plain,
and you took the road back to the harbour, drenched in the summer storm.

Song, For Petro

On Pelion, among the chestnut trees

What moves, though still, yet sounds,
   what, breathing, blows mysterious,
perfuming this whole valley
   channelling mountain waters
to race and tumble, child-like,
   down to your beach, through memory,
and plunge into the sea – this gift,
   old friend, is yours:
let nobody take it from you.

What appetite, unearthly,
   for speech, which makes men human,
and music, which makes men gods,
   to devour the core of the world
and rivet your huge frame
   to this land, this light, this people,
returning again and again – this gift,
   old friend, is yours:
let nobody take it from you.

What chains you to rocky roads
   towards that village square,
Where you'll sit and drink white wine
   with friends under the plane tree
all night, for the *Panaghiá,*
   then weep by the sea at sunrise
behind the blue island – this gift,
   old friend, is yours:
let nobody take it from you.

What halts you, timeless, in bars
   in rundown city alleys,
to tower like some statue
   moved only to talk by old men
whose eyes gleam old black light,
   and to hell with the whole business
of the world, fit for fools – this gift,
   old friend, is yours:
let nobody take it from you.

And what Odyssean journey,
   which is itself your home,
earthed origin and starred goal,
   to this mountain's far side,
unexplored, intractable,
   tightens your old heart strings
to laugh, and travel again – this gift,
   old friend, is yours:
nobody can take it from you.

Shell

Still there remains the yellow essence, summer...

The golden giant shell hangs nailed against your wall, more than a little cracked, though you mended it with glue, and drilled two clean holes there for memory's green cord to loop through, and hammered the nail in firmly to make sure it wouldn't fall. Summer has shrunk and dried to an ornament in the hall, souvenir of some place you passed or name you thought you knew, which, like a tarnished mirror, no longer quite shows true, except when faded sea scents come to your recall. Then suddenly the mirror no longer shows your face, but hands enclosing hands over a pebble on a beach, and medusas, starfish, and seagreens, delicate as lace, and an underwater statue of a blonde youth, out of reach, who still may move in dance for you, perfect in poise and grace, and hail you, who have half forgotten, in the sea's secret speech.

Cicadas (II)

. . . the way the cicadas stop suddenly and all together.

They will never stop, these cicadas,
all my life long. Their voices will never
once leave me alone. Sometimes they groan
like the dead, underneath my floorboards,
they whine like the unborn outside my window
or hover, like angels, over the surrounding hills
where, in high pitched voices, they argue my destiny
till their whole assembly has reached its decision
and I can smell them, out there in the darkness.
Even in the north, in winter, I hear them
creaking under snow, breaking up glaciers;
or, roped like slaves, heaving slabs of silence
into pyramids of music to celebrate a pharaoh
across deserts on the ocean's chilly floor.
Always I hear them, relentlessly calling me
from the other side of dreams, from the other
shore of dreams. And I fear them and I love them
as I fear and love dying . . .

Their voices spur me: *Dream more deeply,*
they clamour through night. And they dig in their heels
as they ride me into sleep, leaning closer
over me, touching me with their breasts,
their hands scratching my shoulders as I struggle
to command them, until their palms cup my ears
and I hear my secret sea flood in, my hushed inner sea,
like a child's, listening at the rim of a nautilus,
and gently they haul me in the sea's deepest caves.

Blood, they insist through day, *Sperm. Sweat. Salt.*
Crazy birds chirping, old crones cackling,
village philosophers full of homely wisdom,
bright eyed and red cheeked, children laughing,
they purr, miaow, bark, they whinny, roar and howl:
Write, write, they wail. *Sing with us,* they hum.
Do not forget your origin. The gold sun, they shriek
*is a black apple buried under the lake of darkness
and we its pips, the black seeds of the sun.*

Without them, no sky, no sea, no land, no light,
no wisdom no madness no love no breath
without them no song or poem
No   they will never leave me

In Memory of George Seferis (II)

And if you command me to drink poison, I thank you . . .

Black is the light behind the blaze of day
and dark the core beneath its coloured coat,
Devour it, lest it eat your soul away.

Though bright the moon and clear the Milky Way
in blackest ink their first Creator wrote
Black is the light behind the blaze of day.

Its juice flows in your bloodstream. Do not say
It's poison, and there is no antidote.
Devour it, lest it eat your soul away.

And do not be afraid, though darkness may
turn seas to pitch and skies to creosote.
Black is the light behind the blaze of day.

Its seed lies hidden in you. You're the clay
it grows beneath. It keeps your breath afloat.
Devour it, lest it eat your soul away,

So, take this apple. Eat it. Why dismay?
Its taste is sweet, although it sear your throat.
Black is the light behind the blaze of day.
Devour it, lest it eat your soul away.

Ambassador
(An Old Man in the Harbour)

The first thing God made is the long journey

You'll come out and greet me underneath the plane tree, shake my hand warmly, spread your palm on my back, and guide me safely across the wide avenue, where we'll sit at a shaded table on the whitewashed pavement: you, dressed in your light suit with the old baggy trousers, puffing the same worn pipe I've seen in your photographs, and the dog following you, curling in a doze; and I, tired and unshaven after my long journey, to find you out at last, to see you at all costs in the town where you live, located with some difficulty, its name being absent from maps in my language.

And you'll ask if I have eaten; and I, who'll really want to say, 'Old man, I love you,' will smile and offer a banal, polite disclaimer; and you'll tilt your big body back in the wooden chair, and say to the waiter, who'll have appeared from nowhere, '*Káli spéra, Táki, fére éna ikosipendáriko yiá to fílo mou ethó, kaí yiá ména mía bíra. Kaí káti mezedákia, ópos nomízis, vévaia – thalassiná, ómos.*' ('Good evening, Taki, bring a 25 drachma flask for my friend here, and a beer for me. And some bits and pieces too, whatever you think best – but sea food of course.') And to the table he'll bring a small flask of *tsipouro*, iced water and a beer; and then, one after the other, dishes of fresh crayfish, crab, oysters, mussels, prawns, ringed octopus, grilled squid, anchovies, sardines, olives, and a mixed salad with *féta*. And you'll sigh, put your pipe in the ashtray, unfold a white napkin and rub your hands together: 'Yes, we Ionians know how to enjoy ourselves. This reminds me of old times, before 'twenty two . . .'

And then, perhaps, I'll stammer, 'Although, you know, we never met, before, I've walked your favourite streets – Syngróu, Panepistimíou – and even though you were long gone, I've visited the house you lived in when you were a guest in my own country. And now at last I've found you, here in your own place . . .'

And you'll lean forward, quiet-eyed, smiling, and say, '*Akóu pethí mou* ('Listen my friend' lit. 'Listen, my child'): I found my way to this harbour, and knew it for home, only when this mongrel yapped at me. And I'd been gone years and lost all my best companions: some disappeared suddenly, some were drowned at sea, some emigrated and never wrote letters home; some died in the north, and some in Turkey, Egypt, Cyprus . . . I don't recall every name, but still I hear all their voices, and see each one of their faces just as if they were sitting with us now. If it hadn't been for them, calling me across years from other distant islands, I'm sure I'd never have set out in the first place. They gave me hope and courage. Their hope *was* my courage. And just as then, so now . . . But, forgive me. Shall we enjoy this fine spread? Tell me, are people over there still much the same?'

And I'll say, simply, 'Yes,' and we'll clink glasses together, toasting life, and memory, and each thinking of those we love; and you'll point out a very old man at another table, intent over a book, a glass of wine before him: 'Remember the one who said, What's the use of poets in a mean-spirited age? – that's him, sitting there. He was already here long before I arrived, and here he will stay, like me. No doubt his memory will long outlast mine . . . But how about you? Have you much farther to travel?' Maybe then I'll tell you something of my place in the hills, which I haven't seen in years and wept when I last left it, which still today, as then, is an occupied city. But I shan't go into detail: it will be time to go. You will insist on paying, and I'll thank you

for the meal and your hospitality; and we'll shake hands again,
and agree, without fail, some other summer, to meet and talk
under the same plane tree, and then you'll walk away, my gentle
ambassador, to the centre of the town, the mangy dog at your
heels, muttering,

> 'Of all the names, of all the dead I loved,
> too many are forgotten who made the same journey . . .',
> your pipe in your mouth again, puffing on it slowly,
> its scent still in my nostrils, like an autumn bonfire,
> and the sun burning a hole in the centre of the bay.

May

As I walk in the garden with Lara and Alexander,
between the dying lilac and opening, first rose,
the air belongs to summer again, and longing.
Pink blossoms are browning and falling. It's May.
The world anoints my whole body in glory,
but I'm not drunk on you yet, world, although I'm trying,
knocking each breath back like a double brandy
because your body's beauty strikes terror through me,
as death blows through the fences, spreading pollen,
and, because my brain keeps back and shoulders firm
against the walls I have built around old sadnesses,
because it thinks becauses, barred in ironies,
and now, as the walls inside me slowly melt,
I don't know where they've gone, the fears I knew
for years and years, and trusted more than gladness,
and want, at once, and do not want this melting
and terror that fall together with blossoms falling,
my poem tries harder not to betray its pain.

Now I'll make you a poem, from lilac, I want
to tell my children. A true story. Lara holds my hand
and Alexander bobs, cradled in the nook of my arm.
Fthah, says Lara, pointing. Does she mean *There*
or *Flower*? And the whole garden opens around her,
you can see it in her wide eyes, as, two years old,
cheeks burning, she toddles to the brink of speech.
and this precise instant, I know I shall remember
the instant itself fixed forever, when we shared the world
whole, in a word, and know also the act of knowing,
hers and mine joined together, will be that memory's core,
far finer formed than in dream time, seen clearer
than in a photograph. Hairs on my forearms stand,

tears brim in my eyes, I shiver in the warmth,
my fantasies are earthed, and all love is fleshed.
And now, the garden opens its soul to me also,
and its whole complex world, like a perfect jar, cracks,
spilling into my head a poem scented with lilac.

Here, children, your poem. But my voice sticks. I say
nothing. The poem's words, unspoken, are too full of pain.
Wrong. Wrong. Lies. The pain in the poem is mine.
This is the month my father broke his heart in.
It cracked. He died. The lilac was in bloom.
In the back room of our quiet North London house
whose French windows opened on another garden,
Israel Alexander Berengarten, musician,
born in Warsaw, brought up in the East End,
singer in seven languages, including Yiddish,
each evening through that spring had played his cello
till long past dark, in tears, his finest concert,
to his daughter Sarah, born deaf, dumb and blind,
to get her to hear, to try to get her to hear
the song of the Swan of Tuonela
moving out through silence over the Black Lake.
Israel Alexander, I'm calling you back in this poem
I want the courage to give my children.

Blind, deaf and speechless to the world, making high-pitched
raucous screams, like an owl, or an owl's prey,
with lolling head, lips drooling, her arms
flailing, contorted, fingers unable to clutch,
his mindless infant daughter broke his spirit.
And one May morning, his forty-sixth birthday,

he stayed in bed, with chest cramps, back pains, toothache,
grumbling at Rosalind, again six months pregnant.
And suffering morning sickness, to answer the doorbell.
A telegram, with flowers. Many Happy Returns.
She waddled back upstairs bearing the light greeting,
but he lay there dead, and one day later
she buried him with his cello bow beside him.
As in a dream, as clear, as in a photograph,
I see his writhing mouth, I hear him calling
through a morning sleek and pregnant with ephemeral
perfume of lilac on the pollen-laden air
and all his thoughts and vessels stop at once.

Now Rosalind sits at her mirror combing out her hair,
hollow-eyed, big-bellied, in a loose smock and slippers,
while her four-year-old son studies her through the glass.
Mummy, he asks, Tell me, when's Daddy coming home?
Quietly she answers, He won't come back. He's dead.
Soon you'll have new baby to play with instead.
And, slowly, as a bow moves over a cello's strings
playing some old lament, she goes on combing her hair
whose delicate perfume reminds the boy of lilac.
Then a girl is born, Alexis. More telegrams. More flowers.
A clan of smiles fills the house. Aunts, uncles, cousins.
Only the empty O of a wooden unplayed instrument
howls still in silence in a corner against the wall.
Israel Alexander – the Greek means Defender of Men,
the boy is soon to learn – will not return again.
Now, thirty years later, Rosalind sleeps by her husband
on the other side of his bow, and Sarah too is dust,
and the aunts and uncles lie low, buried or cremated.

Genealogy and mourning: the language of the Jews.
Ada came, and Alec, Gertrude, and big-souled Bertha,
Dave with his fat cigar and a half-crown for the boy,
Lily, Jacques and Harry, Annie, Rita and Stanley,
huge-hearted Manny, Bessie, and Renée, Frank's wife:
to name each plant that grows, each individual stem
that blossomed, fruited, died, and in turn was seeded
here, in memory's garden, and to forget not one,
is my task and possession, I want to explain
to my children. But still, my voice sticks, and the poem
I wanted to make them and their children's children,
my own accurate testimony of what I knew and loved,
to last, if not forever, longer than my own life,
falters on my tongue, as pain pulls my breath back still.
What need they know of this knowledge, or understand
of this heritage, this litany of sadnesses
borne on the lilac's perfume, whispering through my mind,
where, from every bloom in this garden, I hear ghosts?

Now, walking in this garden, among blossoms falling,
with my own daughter Lara and son Alexander,
I hear my father's music call me from his grave,
and the Swan of Tuonela rises from the lake
to beat its white wings against my shuttered heart.
How shall these dead be honoured, let alone counted?
I ask of the song, and my father's cello replies:
lilac has newly fallen. Now is the time of roses.
wake from your dream. Speak out, to men's hearts and minds.
Wake, and walk out, now, free, into the world
where now your small son coos and babbles as he rides
across this May garden in the crook of your arm
as though you were a chariot he turns like a God

over a Greek heaven, and like another Mab, new risen,
your two-year-old daughter herself culls speech from flowers.
defender of Men, I reply, Here, in this poem
I wanted to make right and stammered long to speak,
play again for the born, and the unborn children.

Here, poem, begin, while still these dream images
are manifest around me, and each one, like a bee,
collects unnumbered memories into my brain cells
gently ushered and hosted by perfumes from flowers,
and, heavy among these houses, fences, walls and wires,
across these English gardens, along these neat avenues
lined with privet and hawthorn, I hear the air hum
with sounds of a deep instrument being stroked unseen
by my father's bow, plucked seasoned from his coffin,
its fibres rubbed silken on the resin of my thought.
I want that sound of his big-bellied cello
with strings well tautened, strong and finely tuned,
rooted and resonant, here, in my poem,
till its chords, huge-hearted, burst as a tree bursts
open in leaf and flower, weaving, interweaving
on air, the scents of summer, lilac and roses,
to shower joy on my children, Lara and Alexander,
and honey of memory be savoured on their tongues.

And here, since love has called me to speak out
across years, through pain, to celebrate in the quiet
words of a poem made in a garden, for children,
the music my father made, amid lilac perfume,
I want that same scent, of sweet almost unbearable
promise of summer, to drown my own self-doubt,

my hard-edged ironies and soft-centred cowardice
with its living body's presence, and so thoroughly
to permeate every filament of this poem
that every word in it will radiate his love.
So now, the poem ends, as *Fthah,* my daughter calls,
in an instant that echoes and shimmers, and the spines
of trees tremble, and a hush falls over the garden,
and this thing, or process, or movement, pours molten
in the well of a word, where it will go on ringing,
spanned by fragile speech, firmed and bell-like always,
impossible to break and made doubly deep and strong
by my father's music which called me from his grave.

Against the Day

Against the Brydale day, which is not long . . .
SPENSER

I

Against the window, against desire, against
expectation, which is not long, she leans

away from her light source, and her eyes
stay just in shadow as she seems to smile

or say hello, before she starts singing
her song which binds unguarded love to you:

against the gold and white fire of her dress,
against a covered, curtain-hidden sun,

she plays it throughout everlastingness,
glowing, a pearl, offset against the day.

II

Against her covered, curtain-hidden sun.
by being just and all she knows she is,

she plays her being's pattern, as she glows
against the day, which settles in her core

and grows there, generous, clear centred, sure,
as if she were some sturdy, dew-pearled rose

gathering light towards her. It collects
within her forehead, pools beneath her skin

and radiates towards us, quiet, strong,
delicate, but untouchable, as her song.

III

This music binds unguarded love to you,
her fingers may say to her instrument's strings

and her melody call to the shadows and gloom
and whoever listens in the next room

at the end of her gaze, we cannot see.
Hello. Hello. Are you there? Can you hear?

And whether she aims to impress or attract
or simply to please, or just doesn't care,

it's subtle, this mooted joy she folds
in her envelope of luminous air.

IV

She is a pearl, offset against the day,
against the twin perfection she knows she is

and the other perfection she leans towards
which is the space gathering between us

from the pools of her densely pupilled eyes
and the few rich, perfect, ornate things

in the room where, smiling, she sits and sings
the silence which frets our history's

lacunae in unheard of, guessed at bars,
and lights against the space she occupies.

V

Delicate, but untouchable as her song,
in playing, she tunes an orchestrated light

which is her being's pattern, and no more
than what she is, or has awareness of.

Smiling, she plays as if her song were willed
by a more intelligent, kinder love

protecting and surrounding her young face
than any we have understanding of,

as if the day itself had overspilled
itself through her to make those fingers skilled.

VI

In her envelope of luminous air,
joy may be folded, and some other things:

pearls round her neck, but no bracelets or rings,
whose absence may mean, imply or suggest

an innocence: in her ringleted hair,
ermine and silk, she is wearing her best,

as she plays on, quiet, aware-unaware
and ready to move yet still seem at rest,

whether she's smiling, or blushing, or sings
and plays for herself, and just doesn't care.

VII

She lights against the space she occupies,
familiar in its elegance and grace,

and yet, in youthful eagerness, her face
leans still against more space, she may not know

outside this screened, framed room she's captured in
against the daylight, closeted for good

in the too pure perfection of a pearl,
against desire, that radiates through her skin:

now, now, she plays, for she is young, a girl
just turning from us into womanhood.

VIII

The day in her, to make her fingers skilled
(as though she were the space she occupies)

to reach across the broken, varnished years
in silent music no-one really hears

towards us in another century,
has made her human: no pure pearl or bloom

could possess such composure. Those deep eyes
are burdened with too fine, alert intelligence

and too prepared, in willing mute obedience
to wait forever in her drawing room.

IX

If she plays for herself, and just doesn't care
whose being she plucks from her instrument's strings

(woman, girl, woman, in yellow and white),
but smiles at an audience of none, in the wings,

no secret admirer, protected from sight,
no parent or guardian to applaud her, or call,

then it's her own selfhood she sifts as she sings
and her own self-becoming wavering there

hidden against the chiaroscuro half-light
as in an unseen mirror on a wall.

X

Just turning from us into womanhood
against the day, against parental praise,

she gives to shadows one half of her face
and a warm human longing fills her gaze

yet quietens it, for it is still uncertain.
so, balanced between action and repose,

she looks away. What there she sees or knows
offstage, in her own private, secret place,

waits there, without embodiment or history
and is not for the telling. It's her mystery.

XI

To wait for ever in her drawing room
could be her destiny, always: poised steady

as a dart to pierce the adulthood
she leans against, but never will command

more than the brush held in her maker's hand
who formed her, against day, against desire

and against his day's possessions. Against
her bridal day, no girl could seem so ready

as she, in certain hope, so qualified
by all but nature, for her womanhood.

XII

As if glimpsed in a mirror on a wall
she's posed, as ornamental as the tree

gilt-framed behind her: nature trapped inside
Artifice, inside artifice, where she,

pearled tracery on rich parental pride,
sits screened in flattened space, to play on three

dimensions, self-contained, in perfect liberty:
but the fourth, our common history, we share

with her across the barricaded years
within whose space alone may she be freed.

XIII

What is not for the telling, but her mystery,
we cannot know: she may play for her groom,

or entertain a friend, or family guest,
who, deep in the interior of her room,

off in the wings, unfettered by her frame,
knows her full repertoire we cannot hear.

we only see her hopeful gaze arrest
on absent presence, distant and yet near,

and whoever may be listening, manifest
space as the sound her silent song must claim.

XIV

From all in nature must her womanhood
remain exempt, unless you hear her. This

is still and always all art ever meant,
and only you have natural power to call

her being from its painted artifice
created by the man who patterned all

he knew in her, of love's integument
against the day. You are the instrument

she plays on, until doomsday: against you
the gloom she gazes, still and always, through.

XV

Within whose space, alone, may she be free
if not in yours? Come, hear her subtle playing

unlock the solid shutters of the years
and open them, light-wrought, in filigree:

playing her being's pattern, she plays true.
she is the song she plays, and what it's saying

(this music wings unguarded love to you),
calls you, who are her song's recipient,

yourself, to pattern love, her music's key,
and join her in the gift of this, her moment.

XVI

Your space: the single sound her song may claim
to open, is the gift a father knew

seeing his natural daughter come of age.
This child of his will meet her adulthood

by playing her being's pattern quietly through
the centuries, until she reaches you.

You are her hope, her natural heritage.
You are the absent audience in her wings.

Your entrance is the cue a parent would
most desire for her. It is for you she sings.

XVII

The gloom she gazes still and always through
clears, as you listen. This, her painter knew:

unless you hear her music, and impress
the sound it makes upon your inner ear,

she will not play at all but wait forever.
she gives herself. Her gift is its own giver

and its envelope of luminous air
bears your mark on it. You are its address.

Whoever you may be, although unknown,
her music plays to all of you alone.

XVIII

Come, join her in the gift of this, her moment,
becoming her own secret audience

as if you were the listener in the wings
for whom her music's made, performed and meant,

and, though this be impossible, confess
how well you hear and understand these songs

she plays to you through everlastingness
on soundless subtle chords no aural sense

could ever pluck, except against the heart,
against the day, against desire, in art.

Croft Woods

I pace Croft Woods beneath a slanted source
of sunlight by a winding river bank.
I stoop, observing mushrooms, mosses, ferns.
and trace their whorls or veins, thickened by rain.
An early autumn afternoon in England,
green, deep and crisp, entirely beautiful.

Swifts wheel before migration. Their screams
beckon to their companions – *Africa!*
Massed cells of blackberries hover on their bushes,
and the ground is strewn with husks, like little mines
bobbing on an irregular green sea,
splitting out conkers, polished to perfection.

The light here hangs diagonally down,
an alphabet of traceries and shadows
I have not learned, but only half intuit.
illiterate, I stumble like a foreigner
who cannot read the simplest of its messages.
but still it daunts me, calls me deep into it.

Blue moss, moonwort, fronded maidenhair,
dusty spores of buckler and hart's-tongue nestling
under cow-grass and nettles, where I tread,
cry for release: *Go soft now and in peace.*
I wish I were a ghost, not to disturb
their roots planted more deeply than our dead.

I thought I heard a rising breeze above
brush leaves, pluck branches – yes, the usual
English lute – Dowland's, Wyatt's, Shakespeare's,
scores so well-known, familiar and loved
no repetition or variant ever could
dull those clear chords against their bowls of wood.

But no, I stop and catch my deepening breath.
Complete silence, or silence magnified,
full of no sound, as in a cave or well,
and I am falling into it, down, down.
I am transparent, empty, bodiless,
the instant past an echo's tadpole-tip –

the second after sound has lost its grip
on sound's reverberation, the exact moment
a tap has been turned off and stops its drip,
or lips are closed and eyes are sealed for ever
and the heart's metronome has petered out,
like sap in winter – all I was has vanished.

I am a shell without a listening child
to hear the sea in. I'm the sea itself
solidified, without a moon to pull
a wind or raise a cloud or comb a wave.
where have I gone – where has my own self gone
out of this everlasting-seeming pause?

I stop and start. And suddenly a swelling
of light behind the day, from day anterior
to light that patterns traceries in eyes,
pours upwards and outswells itself, then cracks
this early evening silence like an eggshell
and a new creature hatches, out of nothing.

Like a waterfall which shatters into droplets,
a music, if it can be called a music,
as if upon a screen that is no screen
throws images that cannot be imagined,
and I'm compelled to listen to another
stranger, eerier music from the forest.

Our speech is built on spirals spun of air,
voice-pillars that support whole architectures
of meanings on their shoulders, caryatids
without whose weight the topless roofs of thought
would crumble and cave in, as mountains might
be one with valleys, on the Day of Judgement.

But in the forest, mother of cathedrals,
in starred, sky-tented glade, in cultured garden,
in orchard, copse or grove, high moor or fen,
curtains dividing speech and silence fall,
and colloquies of oxygen and carbon
counterpoint chants of plants and breaths of men.

And these translucent symphonies of sap
print negatives of speech, gaps, absences,
unstitching and unweaving human voices
to dim inverted echoes of our origins,
as shimmering escarpments, cliffs and peaks
reflect in lakes through which the abyss speaks.

On still lake surfaces lie twin perspectives,
both open simultaneously to view:
what seems, reflected by superior light,
and all that really lives and moves below.
So, in the fugues of plants we trace both bright
marks of our own world, and a more mysterious glow –

less than an echo's ripple, or the gleam
on eddying water, or light-filament
suddenly dew-decked on a spider's thread,
as if made of another element
spun out, unbroken for us, by the dead,
and stretched to waking from behind the dream.

Now, as from mist that rises when the sun
has dried a level band above the dawn,
a veil is drawn back through me and I wait
for it to billow wide and stretch till torn.
which way? To climb? To dive? *My child, come down!*
I enter in. I do not hesitate.

Unbearable polyphonies! I'm hemmed
on all sides by a shadow-orchestra
playing not sound, but mirrorings of sound,
an anti-music, music's twin and opposite,
fluid in meanings, filled with coded messages
of bodiless bodies, dry dews, airless airs.

Through punning alien non-calls from green stems
they challenge me in murmurs, less than murmurs
untraceable, from the other side of silence,
mysteriously forcing upwards through this ground
orders to stop, to listen, and to stand
chilled by their winds on sounds that have no sound.

Tougher than taproots, lacier than branches,
this music bids me recognise the innumerable
dead, who stretch up moistly pleading hands
towards me, beckoning, taunting me to enter
through scented lips and fingertips of plants
their watery realm of uncreated gardens.

Come down, come down, protected from the wind
that howls over the world from dusk till dawn.
surround yourself with music underpinned
by currents in the earth, not of this air.
Pass, through the gates of ivory and horn,
unchained alike from hope, fear and despair.

*Come down, come down, beneath the plough and furrow
where no bat dives and spider never clambers,
to wreathe old skulls in webs or nest in marrow
under memorial slabs or tombstone lids.
come roam our tunnelled corridors and chambers
carved deeper far than cores of pyramids.*

*Come, be the dragon, vigilant through sleep,
who guards the dungeon-treasure in the keep,
a carpenter locked in damp airless rooms
whose roof-rafters are coffins, attics graves,
come and be sentry to these catacombs,
the minotaur of labyrinthine caves.*

Here is a music culled from peat and loam
in swamp or marsh, and hollows under hills
where skulls of slaves and outlaws have been tossed.
Here is a score penned under frozen taiga
where mammoth bones are packed in permafrost
alongside undiscovered minerals.

And listening to this music is descending
a ladder dangling in an endless void,
to reach its end, let go, and still to tumble
throughout one's self until all self is blown
like breath from dying lungs or a balloon,
and further fall, a meteoric stone.

Deeper than self entirely, made transparent,
the dreamer enters unsleep, a new zone,
and in so doing, *climbs*! If this is falling,
it is a falling upwards, a dawn breaking
a dream undreamed, redressed, a double-waking,
and through fear so far gone, fear is unknown.

Frail leaf, veined with shadow-blood, now I touch you,
I become other, unspeaking, I grow down
into your zone of no-time, before time-was,
pay my obol entry to join your dream-cast,
and recall formless forms from which this world's
definitive solid shapes are sculpted statues.

I touch a world inside the veins of rock
which Michelangelo knew before he chiselled
to dig from them his perfect Rondanini.
I trace the clouded face of the Madonna,
I'm Goethe's Faust, descending, past the Mothers,
and the stone-carver of Dolní Vestoníce.

I fall to before Adam. Is this sleep?
No serpent in the grass can do me harm.
My child, come deeper inwards. Do not weep.
I hibernate with squirrels under snows.
I am at one with Keats and Mandelstam,
I am the bloodless blood inside the rose.

I follow tracks of grubs and centipedes,
I burrow tunnels hewn by humble worms,
I shrink and swell with water, among seeds;
my world is made of tubers, bulbs and corms,
surrounded by their strings, drums, bells and horns
under green mossy banks and grassy lawns.

Shall I root, like the cone of a sequoia
and grow, encircled by a ring of daughters,
and when I am a henge of dusky coal,
and milky sap's solidified in amber,
turn fossil carbon back to living wood
where bees, extinct, make honey from dead flowers?

And now, I have the key – of songs perpetual
accompaniments to our own human music,
in ebbing undertow and swelling currents
reaching deeper beneath than birds above,
more various than blackbird, thrush or field-lark,
or nightingale's outpourings in dark gardens.

Here is the score, and now I have the words –
prelude, crescendo, finale, strewn from silences
that lie behind dumb sources of the wind.
This song of plants builds tuned keys for the chords,
threads to the maze, and figures to the dance,
scales to the stars – and scaffolds to mortality.

These boughs and trunks are valves the underworld
allows the dead we tread on underfoot
to breathe a little through from atmospheres
funnelled from earthy moistures. Each porous
bulb, root, tuber is a well sprung door
hinged between death and life and keyed by dream.

Withstanding stresses higher than our hopes,
through hollowed pipes which subtly coil and bend
on stems stretched taut, to analyse and parse
galactic grammars without start or end,
blossoms and flowers, like astral telescopes,
in petalled bowls snatch impulses from stars.

Is this the way for sure? I cannot know
but trust and follow one direction, down,
deepening through darkness. There, may another light,
agleam, then brightening like a shooting star
shattered on ruffled waters of pale lake
through this world's clouded margins, break and shine.

Though rainbows, ribboned evenings, arrowed twilights
and orchestras of summer afternoons
in greeny plaited mazes wreathe light hours
and blind me to that ever-other kingdom,
still may these voices wake me, interwoven
through trees and shrubs, with scents of herbs and flowers.

As for the birds that wheel among upon these trees
surrounding me, and call to their companions,
they'll be my questioned questioners, not masters,
my frank inquisitors, and testers of my spirit.
We shall migrate like them, on beating air,
and suddenly be no longer anywhere.

What love I bear you, world, I cannot vow
to promises, allurements, wedding rings
of human projects cast in mere futurities.
If love is to be filled it must be now
by trusting in the heights *and* depths of things.
Love cannot grow, die, be reborn. *It is.*

Mirrors of music: see how here I go
down, inward, through impenetrable shells
of silences, through silence, into silence.
Towers of Babel, walls of Jericho
tumble to petalled trumpets, pollen bells
of flowers strung on unfathomable wells.

Spectres of blossoms, cloudy petal fluff
and wind-tossed seeds thrown feathered from their husks
play melodies that can't be tracked on air.
Chords brushed from nothing, plaited lacy stuff,
chains out of nowhere, cables combed from void,
join death to us across their bridge of hair.

Conundrums of falling leaves, brushed honey-gold,
cyclamen, autumn crocus, moss and mould,
print coded passwords on my lips that yet
are steeped and webbed in dew, still freshly wet.
These voices call from zones where dews have dried
and guiding hope and love rest purified.

Vasilissa

My whole body aches from our lovemaking but I want you more more. You have utterly exhausted me drained my core away transplanted yours in its place. I am some rattling winnowed husk but still I can't have enough of you. Again I want your body closeted tight around me. Again I want your limbs clustered around mine. Again I want your tongue in my mouth my lips lapping your lips your kind inspiring hands cupping and cradling my soul. Again I want your tender heart beating against my side. Lord knows I can hardly believe this We have only just met Explain to me what's happening I want your whole *being* wrapped wholly around mine.

I want to sit in your kitchen and listen to you unravelling each inch of your life story in slow elaborate detail as you chain-smoke your little roll-ups. I want to drink your smile the dimples turning to creases around your quiet lips and the amber reticence in your warm amazing eyes. I want to spend days and nights with you smiling in total nakedness never answering the phone. I want to cook banquets for you learn your swift clattering recipes stroke your elegant neck and help you wash your hair. I want to shower your belly stroke the curls in your hollows caress your silver moans.

I want to buy you lilies feast in luxurious restaurants fuck you on deserted beaches introduce you to my family and best oldest friends. I want to go travelling with you rediscover the ruined places reconsecrate the heart's abandoned and wasted synagogues. I want you to tell me how to rearrange my furniture tease me out of my blindspots narrownesses and pomposities and not mind too much if I take photographs of you and paint you.

I want to kiss your old-young voice echoing our common ancestors. Their hopes aches dreams tremblings their kabbalistic fire.

The merest scent of your voice peals fire bells in through around me. Do you know nobody ever has rung them quite like this before. I never knew they could echo such wholehearted harmonies, so simply and clearly. My eyes dissolve to pools every time you glance at me. Your smile surrounds and enters me like forest air or birdsong. Your dark name murmurs the innerings and mirrorings of mandalas. Why is it I hear the hum of innumerable bees. Oh is there just a chance a small gate hidden

in this moment that might creak open a little, wide enough to admit me. That I too could be called, even be considered worthy. Live clean and good, quell fear and doubt, rest calm in decent justice. In such a temple as this I've longed to praise and worship. Your complex mind, glory. Your baffling body, radiance. Your presence, necessity. Your companionship, destiny. In your depths, delight. But in your tenderness, terror. Daughter of my own ancestors – Vasilissa – what scope or space is there for you to let me love you. Heart don't crack from excess of peace and joy.

Postscript and Notes

Postscript

The following pages include information on dates and places of composition, contexts, dedications, some textual references, and reprinted notes from earlier editions of some of the poems.

The first edition of this collection appeared in 2004 under the name Richard Burns. In changing my authorial name to Richard Berengarten, I have repossessed the name of my father, Alexander Berengarten.

This edition of *For the Living* also makes several changes in content. Since its first edition, the publication of four further volumes in the *Selected Writings* series has enabled me to transfer three poems into the contexts they were originally intended for: 'The Ballad of the Seagull' and 'Wayside Shrine' have been included in *The Blue Butterfly* (volume 3), and 'The Voice in the Garden' in *Under Balkan Light* (volume 5). I have added two uncollected texts, written in the 1970s and 1980s respectively: 'The Offence of Poetry' and 'Day Estate'. As in the first edition of *For the Living*, the long poem, *The Manager* (Elliott & Thompson, 2001) is excluded: *The Manager* is now reprinted as volume 2 of the *Selected Writings*. Similarly, *In a Time of Drought* (first published by Shoestring Press, Nottingham, 2005) is reprinted as volume 4. The sequences contained in *Book With No Back Cover* (David Paul, London, 2003) are excluded too, as are all my shorter poems that are not part of sequences.

RB
CAMBRIDGE
SEPTEMBER 2008

Notes

THE EASTER RISING 1967, pp. 1–14
Written in Thebes, in the days immediately following the coup d'état on 21 April 1967. The poem was sent to England via a courier, under the pseudo-Greek pseudonym 'Agnostos Nomolos': i.e. anomalously-unknown-backwards-spelt Solomon. It first appeared as a poster glued into the January 1968 issue of *The London Magazine*. The editor, Alan Ross, wrote: 'In the small hours of the morning of April 21, 1967, just before the Greek Easter, a military Junta took over the Greek government. All transport and communications came to a standstill, censorship and martial law were enforced, and any possible opposition was immediately stifled. In spite of the recent Cyprus eruption, almost universal resentment at home, and criticism abroad, it has somehow managed to keep its hold, calling itself The National Government. *The Easter Rising* was written during Easter week of 1967, during the first days after the coup, by a young Greek poet who calls himself Agnostos Nomolos. The poem has come into our possession after being smuggled out of Greece during the early days of December.'

The fiction of the author's Greek identity was maintained: I presented myself as the poem's translator. Many London literati fell for this, including several Greeks and Anglo-Greeks, even though they may well have had their suspicions.

ACTAEON, pp. 15–21
Written in 1965–6, Venice.

AVEBURY, pp. 23–50
Written in Great Shelford, 1971. Dedicated to Octavio Paz. An Italian translation by Roberto Sanesi was published by La Nuova Foglio, Macerata, 1976. A Greek version has been made by Paschalis Nikolaou.

From the afterword to the first edition, 1973
I should like to record my thanks to those who, knowingly or unknowingly [. . .] have helped or influenced me in the composition and correction of this poem: first, for their criticism, their encouragement, and above all their example as poets, to Peter Russell and Octavio Paz. If I had not first read the former's unpublished *Ephemeron* and the latter's *Blanco* and *Sun Stone* (*Piedra de Sol*) I doubt if *Avebury* would have got written. Then, to the unknown poet or poets who composed *The Epic of Gilgamesh*, to G. R. Levy for her book *The Gate of Horn*, and to C. G. Jung, Mircea Eliade and Claude Levi-Strauss for the works of theirs I have read and learnt from.

Added in 2008
G. R. Levy's book is subtitled 'a study of the religious conceptions of the stone age, and their influence upon European thought' (Faber and Faber, London, 1968). The translation of *The Epic of Gilgamesh* I used was by Nancy K. Sandars (Penguin Books, London, 1960). Another key influence was Charles Olson's *The Maximus Poems*.

Epigraphs
Sabbath Morning Service, in *Forms of Prayer for Jewish Workshop*, Vol 1, ed. Ministers of the West London Synagogue of British Jews, Oxford University Press, 1931, p. 15.

Heraclitus, 'On the Universe', fragment CXXIII, in *Hippocrates*, vol, IV, tr. W. H. S. Jones, Loeb Editions, William Heinemann and Harvard University Press, 1967, p. 507.

Octavio Paz, *The Labyrinth of Solitude* (*El Laberinto de la Soledad*), tr. L. Kemp, Allen Lane, The Penguin Press, London, 196, p. 162.

Sections 6–11, pp. 30–35. Five sonnets on seven sculptures:
p. 30, the 'Venus of Willendorf', c. 26,000 B.C., Museum of Natural History, Vienna; and see G. R. Levy, *The Gate of Horn*, pp. 56–63.

p. 31, one of Michelangelo's 'Prisoners', Galleria dell' Accademia, Florence.

p. 32, the 'Winged Victory' of Samothrace, Louvre.

p. 33, two *phalloi* on the island of Delos, shrine of Apollo.

p. 34, two statues in Cycladic marble, Greek National Museum, Athens: a male figure playing a double flute and a harp player, from the island of Keros, c. 2,600–2,400 B.C. For the first of these, see also my *Double Flute* (Enitharmon Press, London, 1972, p. 43). The last two lines of this poem echo Nikos Gatsos' poem 'Amorgos', VI, tr. Edmund Keeley and Philip Sherrard, *Four Greek Poets* (Penguin Books, London, 1966, p.99).

In sections 13–14 (pp. 38–39) and Sections 21 and 23 (pp. 46 and 49), some of the embedded references are to *The Epic of Gilgamesh*, especially to Enkidu, the wild man, and the temple priestess. They also draw material from G. R. Levy, *The Gate of Horn*, especially 'The Cave as Habitation and Sanctury', pp. 3–28. Section 15 (p. 35) refers to Botticelli's 'The Birth of Venus'.

ANGELS, pp. 51–56
Written in Great Shelford between 1974 and 1976. Translated into Serbo-Croat by Bogdana G. Bobić, *Književnost*, Belgrade, 1987.
   p. 55. Tiphareth: the sixth of the ten *Sephiroth* in the Kabbalistic Tree of Life. The line 'sons and daughters of the starry heavens' embeds a reference to a Mesopotamian creation hymn: see N. K. Sanders, *Poems of Heaven and Hell from Ancient Mesopotamia*, (Penguin Books, London, 1971). The final phrase, 'and there is no more sea', derives from *Revelations*, 21:1.

ODE ON THE END OF THE THIRD EXILE, pp. 57–63
Written in Great Shelford and Cambridge around 1976–8. Dedicated to Henry Stamper.
   Section 1, p. 59, and line 1 'double flute': see p. 34 above, line 3, and *Double Flute* (Enitharmon Press, London, 1972) p. 43. Section 3, p. 61, line 2: see Jonah, 1:6. Section 5, p. 63, lines 2–4: *Jonah*, 2:5–6.

NAMING THE CREATURES, pp. 65–69
Written, late 1970s, Great Shelford. Dedicated to the memory of Veronica Forrest-Thompson (1947–1975), and to John Matthias. For p. 67, lines 1 ff: see John Keats: 'Ode to A Nightingale'.

THE OFFENCE OF POETRY, pp. 71–89
Written in Great Shelford, 1973. Influenced by the writings of Martin Buber, especially *I and Thou*, and Heracleitus. Its first publication (in *Littack* IIII, Epping, in the same year) was presented as an invited response to a text by William Oxley entitled 'The Vitalist Memorandum' (*Littack* II, Epping, 1972), but with my distancing preface. Not republished until its inclusion here, 2008.
   pp. 81 and 85: 'the mad eye of the fourth person singular' echoes Lawrence Ferlinghetti's poem 'He'.
   p. 81: 'whither wilt thou fly' echoes George Herbert's 'The Forerunners' in *The Temple*.

THE ROSE OF SHARON, pp. 91–96
The Rose of Sharon is the *Shekhinah*, the feminine aspect of the divine

presence in the Kabbalah. Epigraph from William Blake, 'A Song of Liberty'. Written in Cambridge around 1972–3, in response to Gershom Scholem's *Major Trends in Jewish Mysticism* (Thames and Hudson, London, 1955). Winner of the Keats Memorial Prize, 1974. Translated into Italian by Roberto Sanesi, *Almanacco internazionale dei poeti*, La Pergola, Pesaro, 1975.

Ys, pp. 97–103
Written in Great Shelford, early 1970s. All that survives of a sequence based on the Breton legend.

TRANSFORMATIONS, FROM RIMBAUD'S *LES ILLUMINATIONS*, pp. 105–116
Written in Cambridge, 1985–7. A tribute to Frances Richards (1 August 1901–14 February 1985), who published her colour lithographs for Rimbaud's *Les Illuminations* with the Curwen Press in 1975. Her prints are transformations of Rimbaud's poems and commentaries on them. Some of these poems in turn transform and comment on both Rimbaud's prose-poems and Frances' lithographs, four of which are reproduced *en face*, in black and white.

'Awakening', p. 110, line 6: see Thomas Wyatt's poem: 'They fle from my that sometyme did me seke.'

TREE, pp. 117–130
Written in Cambridge, 1978–9. Dedicated to Gerda Boyeson (1922–2005) and David Boadella. The poem is, among other things, a response to Anne Waldman's chant poem, *Fast Speaking Woman* (City Lights Books, San Francisco, 1975). The epigraph is by Carl Gustav Jung. 'Basilides of Alexandria' was the name Jung gave to the inner voice who, he said, 'dictated' his *Septem Sermones ad Mortuos* (tr. H. G. Baynes, Stuart & Watkins, London, 1961), although Basilides was also a real historical figure. Published translations are: *Arbol*, tr. Clara Janés, Papeles de invierno, Madrid, Spain, 1986; *Baum*, tr. Theo Breuer, Kall-Sistig, 1986; and 'Drvo', tr. Bogdana G. Bobić, *Književnost*, Belgrade, 1987.

Note to first edition, 1981
This poem, *Tree*, has the same number of lines as a year has days. This makes it three lines longer than the height in feet of the tallest tree in the world, the coast Redwood Howard Libbey Tree in Humboldt State Park, California.

Added in 2003
The Californian tree should have caught up by now.

DAY ESTATE, pp. 131–146
Written in Great Shelford and Cambridge during the 1980s. A twelve-part set of variations on the Canonical Hours, composed in honour of Margaret Thatcher and published, nearly thirty years later, in 2008, in recognition of the enduring heritage and legacy of Thatcherian Conservatism, which is still apparently considered fit for purpose throughout the United Kingdom of Great Britain and Northern Ireland.

The epigraph, p. 131, is from Abel Meeropol's poem 'Strange Fruit', made famous by Billie Holliday. Meeropol wrote it in New York, 1937, after seeing a photograph of the lynching of Thomas Shipp and Abram Smith.

In 'Compline', p. 145, line 3 echoes the English nursery rhyme 'Ride a cock horse to Banbury Cross / See a fine lady upon a white horse.' In line 9, 'Make haste to town' refers to the title and chorus of an aria from Henry Purcell's *Dido and Aeneas*. Line 13 yokes two echoes: Walter de la Mare's poem 'Peacock Pie' and the song 'Pie in the sky when you die' by Joe Hill and Woody Guthrie.

'Privileged Octaves' p. 146: the sequence ends as it began with an echo of Billie Holliday, 'Lady Day', especially the lines 'You make me feel so sad. / You make me think of the things I never had.'

BLACK LIGHT, pp. 147–176
Written in Cambridge, Summer 1982. Dedicated to the memory of George Seferis (1900–1971) and for Peter Mansfield (1942–2008). *Black Light* has been translated into: Serbo-Croat (*Crna Svetlost*, tr. Bogdana G. Bobić, Dečje Novine publishers, Gornji Milanovac, 1986); German (*Schwarzes Licht*, tr. Theo Breuer, Bunte Raben Verlag, 1996); Greek (*To Mávro Fós*, tr. Nasos Vayenas & Ilias Layios, Istós Publications, Athens, 2004,); and Slovenian (*Črna svetloba*, Aleph Publishing, Ljubljana, 2004, tr. Ana Jelnikar). The last two of these books include versions of 'Ambassador' as epilogue to the sequence. Three poems from *Black Light* are included in the selection in Spanish, *Las manos y la luz*, translated by Miguel Teruel and Paul S. Derrick, Aula de Poesia 24, Universidad de València, 2008.

Notes to previous English editions, with small changes and additions:
The main passages about 'black light' in Seferis's writings occur in the last section of his long poem *The Thrush*, which he completed in October 1946, and in his journal-entries for the summer of that year. Many of these notes were reworked into the poem. I have drawn heavily from both these sources, and two of the three epigraphs to this sequence come

from them: the long quotation from the end of *The Thrush* is from the translation by Edmund Keeley and Philip Sherrard, in their edition of Seferis's *Collected Poems* (Anvil Press Poetry, London, and Princeton University Press, 1982); and the journal-entry is quoted from the translation by Athan Anagnostopoulos, published under the title *A Poet's Journal 1945–1951* (Harvard University Press, 1975). However, many other passages in Seferis are also relevant, since the theme of 'darkness within light' flows as a constant undercurrent throughout his work. The epigraph from C. M. Bowra is taken from *The Greek Experience* (Mentor Books, 1957, p. 23).

Each of the twelve poems in the sequence has a separate epigraph from Seferis whose source is given below. *The Thrush* provides the majority, but not all, of these. In each case, the epigraph, as well as its surrounding context in the poem it is taken from, operates as a key to my own text. Page references below are to the English text in the bilingual Anvil Press *Collected Poems* (1982 edition), prefaced by the initials GS. In these short epigraphs and in quotations embedded in my own lines, I have followed Keeley's and Sherrard's renderings in most cases, though with some small variations where their rhythms did not match entirely with my own or I wanted to suggest alternative nuances.

An essay by Nasos Vayenas, 'The Genealogy of *The Thrush*' (Chapter IV of his study, *The Poet and the Dancer*, Kedros, Athens, 1979) gave me unexpected new insights, particularly into Seferis's love of Pelion and its importance in his work, and the relationship between *The Thrush* and Eliot's *Four Quartets*.

Greek words are transliterated in the text and glossed below.

'In Memory of George Seferis' (I), p. 153
   Epigraph from *The Thrush*, GS p. 337. This poem won a Duncan Lawrie Prize in the Arvon Poetry Competition, 1982.

'The Voice', p. 154
   Epigraph from section II of The Thrush ('Sensual Elpenor'), GS p. 323; *bouzoúki*: stringed instrument with a bowl like a lute; *baghlamá*: small bouzoúki.

'Soulmonger', pp. 155–156
   The title is the last line of section II of *The Thrush* ('Sensual Elpenor'), GS p. 331; epigraph from 'In the Kyrenia District', GS p. 525; line 17: 'Qelippoth' (pl), lit. 'husks' or 'shells'. In Lurianic Kabbalah, the '[. . .] fragments, together with the sparks of divine light that adhered to them, "fell" into the primordial space.

There they produced in due course the forces of the *qelippah* that fell with them, which are known in kabbalistic terminology as "the other side".' Gershom Scholem, *Sabbatai Ṣevi, The Mystical Messiah 1626–1676*, London, 1973, pp. 33–4 & ff.

'Volta', pp. 157–158
Title: evening promenade; epigraph from 'In the Manner of G. S.', GS p. III: Eleftheria: freedom, and a girl's name.

'Cicadas (I)', p. 159
Epigraph from 'Crickets', GS p. 507, and the last two lines also echo the same poem; *távli*: backgammon; *tsípouro*: an anis drink, like ouzo; *skéto, métno, glykí vrastó*: sugarless, medium, sweet-boiled (terms used for coffee): *nichterídhes*: bats.

'Only the Common Miracle', pp. 160–161
Epigraph from 'Between two bitter moments', GS p. 197.

'Salt', pp. 162–164
Epigraph from *The Thrush*, GS p. 337; *kóre*: maiden, a term used of ancient statuary; '. . . and keeps putting on cassettes of old songs . . .' quoted from Nasos Vayenas, *Biography*, section III, tr. RB (Lobby Press Editions, Cambridge, 1978); *kakaviás*: a fish soup.

'Neolithic', pp. 165–167
Epigraph from 'The Thrush', GS p. 337, with other references in the poem to the same passage, and to Seferis's journal-entries for June 1946.

'Song, for Petro', pp. 168–169
Epigraph from 'In the Manner of G. S.', GS p. 107; *Panaghiá*: The 'All-Holy-One', i.e. The Virgin Mary, whose feast on 15 August occasions all-night celebrations in many villages in Greece; the last line of each verse echoes Yannis Ritsos's long poem *Romiossíni*, which Mikis Theodorakis adapted for a song-cycle with the same title: 'This soil is their soil and our soil – nobody can take it from us.'

'Shell', p. 170
Epigraph from 'A Word for Summer', GS p. 175; see also the line in that poem: 'Still there remains the blonde marble youth, summer.'

'Cicadas (II)', pp. 171–172
Epigraph from the last line of *The Thrush*, GS p. 339.

'In Memory of George Seferis (II)', p. 173
Epigraph from *The Thrush*, GS p. 333.

'Ambassador', p. 174–176
Written in 1985 as epilogue to *Black Light*. Epigraph from GS, p. 287. Previously unpublished in English, but included in the Greek and Slovenian editions of *Black Light* (*To Mávro Fós*, tr. Nasos Vayenas & Ilias Layios, Istós Publishers, Athens, 2004; and *Črna svetloba*, tr. Ana Jelnikar, Aleph Publishing, Ljubljana, 2004).

MAY, pp. 177–184
For Lara Sophia Burns, Alexander Peter Carey (Gully) Burns and Alexis Jennifer Burns; and in memory of Alexander Israel Berengarten, known as Burns (10 May 1901–10 May 1947), and Rosalind Burns, née Schneiderman, known as Taylor (31 October 1911–20 October 1968). Written in Cambridge in the mid-1980s. 'The Swan of Tuonela': title of the third of Sibelius's *Lemminkäinen* symphonic poems.

AGAINST THE DAY, pp. 185–195
A poem in 18 sections, written for Lara Burns on her 18th birthday (7 February 1968). Epigraph from Edmund Spenser's 'Prothalamion'. The poem is also a commentary on 'The Guitar Player' by Jan Vermeer, in Kenwood House, Hampstead. The figure in this painting is said to be Vermeer's daughter. See Edward A. Snow, *A Study of Vermeer* (University of California Press, Berkeley and Los Angeles, 1979).

CROFT WOODS, pp. 197–209
Completed in Cambridge in 1998–9. Influenced by readings of two books by James Hillman, *Revisioning Psychology* (Harper & Row, New York, 1975) and *The Dream and the Underworld* (Harper & Row, New York, 1979). Dedicated to Peter Russell (16 September 1921–22 January 2003).

p. 205, 'Rondanini': the name of Michelangelo's last *Pietà*, in the Sforza Castle, Milan; 'Dolní Vestoníce', site of the statuette of a female figure, c. 27,000 years old, in the Brno museum.

VASILISSA, pp. 211–214
Written in London, 1998; revised, Ballyhealy, 1999.

RB
CAMBRIDGE
SEPTEMBER 2004 & JULY 2008